Child-Rearing Concepts:
Historical Sources

Primary Sources In American History

CONSULTING EDITOR
Grady McWhiney, Wayne State University

IMPERIALISTS VERSUS ANTI-IMPERIALISTS:
The Debate Over Expansionism in the 1890's
Edited by **Richard E. Welch, Jr.**

AMERICAN UTOPIANISM
Edited by **Robert S. Fogarty**

SLAVERY IN AMERICA:
Theodore Weld's *American Slavery As It Is*
Edited by **Richard O. Curry**
and **Joanna Dunlap Cowden**

OVER THERE:
European Reaction to Americans in World War I
Edited by **Robert C. Walton**

CHILD-REARING CONCEPTS:
Historical Sources
Edited by **Philip J. Greven Jr.**

VICTORIAN CULTURE IN AMERICA
Edited by **H. Wayne Morgan**

CHILD-REARING

CONCEPTS, 1628-1861

HISTORICAL

SOURCES

PHILIP J. GREVEN, JR.
RUTGERS UNIVERSITY

F. E. PEACOCK PUBLISHERS, INC.
ITASCA, ILLINOIS

JOHN W. CAUGHEY, Advisory Editor

For Hannah and Jan

Table of Contents

Foreword

It is not easy to understand the past. A good textbook helps by providing what its author — usually a distinguished historian — considers the essential facts and his interpretation of those facts. A good instructor also helps. But the student, if he is to be other than a parrot, must be exposed to more than one or two viewpoints. Told that authorities disagree, the student is likely to ask: "But which interpretation is right?"

At that point he is ready to do some research himself — to read and to evaluate what certain persons who actually saw an event wrote about it. Sampling original sources on which historical interpretations are based is not only an exciting experience; it adds flavor to knowledge. Furthermore, it encourages the student to weigh conflicting evidence himself and to understand historical variety and complexity.

The Primary Sources in American History series provides the documents necessary to explore the past through the eyes of those who lived it. Edited and introduced by an able scholar, each volume in the series contains contemporary material on some historical topic or period — either a collection of varied sources (letters, diaries, memoirs, reports, etc.), or a new edition of a classic eyewitness account.

Grady McWhiney
Editor

Acknowledgment

I wish to acknowledge with gratitude the generous financial assistance received from the Rutgers University Research Council, part of which was used to provide xerox copies of documents used in this volume.

Introduction

Historians study the lives and personalities of adults, but usually pay scant attention to the early formative years of childhood, to informal educational experiences, and to the familial influences that have conditioned those they are attempting to understand. It has been left to other disciplines — anthropology, sociology, and psychology — to demonstrate the profound significance of infancy, childhood, and youth in shaping adult personalities and to analyze the impact of various kinds of child-rearing practices upon the larger culture and society in which individuals and families live. Fortunately, historians in recent years have begun at last to recognize the critical importance of both childhood and familial experiences in their understanding of many aspects of social history.

It also has become clear during the past decade that the historical background of childhood and the family is vital to any understanding of the history of education, since most education prior to the mid-19th century was primarily informal and domestic rather than institutionalized in schools. In the 17th, 18th, and early 19th centuries, education was largely thought of in terms of religious and moral training or of character formation, and only incidentally in terms of formal scholarly training. Education and the history of childhood and the family are inseparably related, as has been demonstrated by several notable studies of the history of education in early America, particularly Bernard Bailyn's

Education in the Forming of American Society (Chapel Hill, 1960), Lawrence A. Cremin's *American Education: The Colonial Experience, 1607–1783* (New York, 1970), and James McLachlan, *American Boarding Schools: A Historical Study* (New York, 1970). Ironically, this sophisticated view is precisely the one espoused consistently by the early writers on education and the family included in this volume.

During the past decade, the history of children and of families in preindustrial Europe has been illuminated by several exceptionally stimulating and provocative studies. The outlines of some of the general developments in the nature and the functioning of French and Dutch families from the late Middle Ages to the early 19th century have been delineated in the brilliant study by Philippe Ariès, *Centuries of Childhood: A Social History of Family Life* (New York, 1962). Peter Laslett's *The World We Have Lost* (New York, 1965) and Alan MacFarlane's *The Family Life of Ralph Josselin, A Seventeenth-Century Clergyman: An Essay in Historical Anthropology* (Cambridge, England, 1970) provide fascinating insights into familial experiences and the social worlds of 17th-century Englishmen. David Hunt's *Parents and Children in History: The Psychology of Family Life in Early Modern France* (New York, 1970) permits comparison with the English studies and also offers a different approach to the interdisciplinary study of the family. These studies of European families are indispensable for the perspectives they provide upon the experiences of children and families in America from the 17th century to the present.

Families in colonial America have been analyzed in a number of historical studies. Edmund S. Morgan's *The Puritan Family: Religion & Domestic Relations in Seventeenth-Century New England* (rev. ed.; New Yrok, 1966) has become a classic study of early American families based upon literary sources. More recently, John Demos's *A Little Commonwealth: Family Life in Plymouth Colony* (New York, 1970) probes many vital aspects of households and the life cycles of families in 17th-century Plymouth, drawing upon analytical models from social psychology and especially from the writings of Erik Erikson. Philip J. Greven, Jr.'s, *Four Generations: Population, Land, and Family in Colonial Andover, Massachusetts* (Ithaca, N.Y., 1970) reflects a very different approach to the history of the family, emphasizing the changing character of familial experience during the 17th and 18th centuries, as demographic factors altered and patriarchalism declined in effectiveness. Both Demos and Greven conclude their studies with general essays on the changing nature of the family in America.

For the history of child rearing, education, and the family in the late 18th and the early 19th centuries, several important studies can be consulted. Monica Kiefer's examination of *American Children through Their Books, 1700–1835* (Philadelphia, 1948) provides a useful general picture of childhood as envisaged by writers of the period. Anne L. Kuhn's *The Mother's Role in Childhood Education: New England Concepts, 1830–1860* (New Haven, 1947) is filled with information and is still one of the best studies of child rearing and the family in the first half of the 19th century. Bernard Wishy's *The Child and the Republic: The Dawn of Modern American Child Nurture* (Philadelphia, 1968) is interesting, too. Peter G. Slater's recent dissertation, "Views of Children and of Child Rearing during the Early National Period: A Study in New England Intellect" (University of California at Berkeley, 1970), is an important analysis of the different traditions of child rearing both in Europe and America. The analysis by Charles Strickland of "A Transcendentalist Father: The Child-Rearing Practices of Bronson Alcott," *Perspectives in American History* (1969), Vol. III, pp. 5–73, provides a fascinating contrast to the views espoused by many of the writers included in this volume.

The literature dealing with child rearing and the family in disciplines other than history is vast, and several studies are particularly valuable. Erik Erikson's study of *Childhood and Society* (New York, 1950) has exerted a powerful influence upon the thought of many young historians, who have found his analysis of the human life cycle and of identity useful in their own analyses of human behavior in the past. Among Erikson's studies that explore varying aspects of childhood and youth are *Young Man Luther: A Study in Psychoanalysis and History* (New York, 1958) and "Identity and the Life Cycle: Selected Papers," in *Psychological Issues,* Vol. I (1959) pp. 18–166. Bruno Bettelheim's study, *The Children of the Dream: Communal Child-Rearing and American Education* (New York, 1969) provides a fascinating perspective upon contemporary methods of child rearing. The general analysis of various kinds of upbringing and their impact upon behavior and personality in *Child Training and Personality: A Cross-Cultural Study* (New Haven, 1953), by John W. M. Whiting and Irvin L. Child, ought to be read in conjunction with the historical sources included in this volume.

Although these sources span a period of more than two centuries, a careful reading of them will demonstrate a remarkable degree of continuity in the assumptions, methods, and goals of the writers, most of whose religious positions locate them within the broad confines of the Puritan-Evangelical tradition. Despite their many differences, these writers share a common concern with controlling and suppressing the autonomy of their children. This preoccupation transcends both time and space and appears with striking repetitiveness even today. For all of these writers, it was evident that particular child-rearing practices and a moral education were fundamental to the achievement of a particular kind of Christian experience in adulthood. When the extent to which their views were maintained decade after decade, century after century, in both England and New England is taken into account, it is easier to understand how their cultural values and their religious beliefs and practices were transmitted successfully from generation to generation.

Alternatives to the Puritan-Evangelical modes of child rearing developed slowly in the colonies during the 18th century, but by the 1820's and 1830's a shift in emphasis away from repression and toward fostering the development of independence in children was evident, even among some of the evangelicals. Not until the mid-19th century, with the publication of Horace Bushnell's *Christian Nurture,* did this transformation gain widespread support and begin to become dominant, but a concern for people who indulged or spoiled their children or exerted insufficient effort toward the repression of their wills at an early age could be noted even in the 17th- and 18th-century writings of Puritans and evangelicals.

Perhaps, then, more parents than we are presently aware of ignored the advice offered by writers such as those represented in this volume. It is almost impossible to be sure. What is clear, though, is that from the 17th century to the present, people have been concerned about "repression" versus "permissiveness," or "breaking the will" as opposed to "indulgence," with respect to their children and their families.

From generation to generation, the powerful impact which the action and attitudes of parents have upon the formation of their childrens' characters has been recognized. While actual child-rearing practices have varied widely over time, awareness of the importance of the role of parents has been sustained by personal as well as religious and political convictions that demonstrate the interrelationships between child-rearing methods, personality, and adult experience and belief.

Many readers may be surprised, therefore, to discover the remarkably high level of sophistication and perceptiveness evident in these 17th-, 18th-, and early 19th-century writings on childhood and the family. For it is only our own historical naïveté which makes us believe we are unique in our preoccupation with the earliest years of human development. For centuries Christian writers have known the critical importance of childhood in shaping the personalities and the piety of successive generations. Many of the most persuasive modern theories of child development and behavior echo arguments and convictions voiced a century or more ago. Even the behaviorist psychologists will discover some remarkable similarities in premises and practices advocated by some of the writers represented here. Historians and psychologists influenced by Erik Erikson will find ample evidence of earlier patterns of development that augment their contemporary analyses of the human life cycle.

As the documents in this collection demonstrate, men and women in the past often were as self-conscious and as concerned about their methods of child rearing and the long-term significance of their parental activities as any modern reader possibly could be. Their language and values were predominantly religious, whereas ours often are scientific and secular, but the basic concern over the centuries has remained the same: how to raise children in ways satisfactory to both parents and society. Many of their answers to this problem are to be found in the sources below.

I.
PURITAN-EVANGELICAL
CONCEPTS

1. John Robinson:
Of Children and Their Education (1628)

Although John Robinson (1575–1625) chose to remain in Holland rather than join William Bradford and the small company of Puritan Separatists who sailed to the New England wilderness in 1620, he ranked among the leaders of this group. He was their minister and their spokesman, and his views and beliefs were shared by the men and women who first settled in America. Robinson was both educated (at Cambridge University) and articulate. For this reason, his 17th-century observations on education provide a point of departure for the analysis of the attitudes and practices of men and women in England and America with respect to both child rearing and education for at least the following two centuries.

OF CHILDREN AND THEIR EDUCATION

GOD, that made all things good, and blessed them, Gen. i. 28–31, imparted expressly this blessing first to his creatures, capable thereof, that they should increase and multiply in their kind. More especially, God created our first parents, male and female, and blessed them, saying, "Be fruitful, and multiply, and fill the earth." This order then set, he hath preserved to this day, and mankind by it. By this, parents when they are dead, live in their children, as parts of them, and imps[1] taken from their stock, and in special manner, one with them. This oneness God's gracious covenant with the

---

From John Robinson, *New Essays: Or, Observations Divine and Moral . . .* in Robert Ashton (ed.), *The Works of John Robinson, Pastor of the Pilgrim Fathers* (Boston: Doctrinal Tract and Book Society, 1851), Vol. I, pp. 242–50.
[1]Grafts.

faithful and their seed confirms, and commends: blessing even
the godly dead parents in their living children; and so cursing
the wicked in theirs, and that often sundry ages afterwards; as
both the Scriptures, common sense, and experience teach.
Such parents as leave their seed under God's covenant and
blessing, as heirs of their father's piety, as Ambrose said of
Theodosius, provide a good inheritance for them, if they
afterwards by their own rebellion and unthankfulness disinherit not themselves. And a sweet comfort it is to Christian
parents, when they can commend their little ones, living, or
dying into Christ's hands in heaven; who being upon earth
testified both in word and deed, their interest in his blessing.
Matt. xix. 13, 14. "The generation of the upright shall be
blessed: but the posterity of the wicked shall be cut off." Psa.
cxii. 2. And as we judge of the plant or graft, by the stock
whence it was taken, till it be grown able to bring proper fruit,
and that the tree be known by the fruit; so do we of children
by their parents, till coming to years of discretion they choose
their own way. Not that grace is derived by natural generation, but by the supernatural covenant with believers and
their seed, confirmed in Christ; and by godly education on the
parent's part, Gen. xvii. 7–11; Gal. iii. 14–22; which promise
of blessing, as it is ever effectual in some, according to the
election of grace, Rom. xi. 5; so where it follows not, usually
the negligence and indulgence of the parents, and, always, the
parties' proper rebellion is the cause thereof; as we may see,
both in the Word of God and daily experience. We read of
Dionysius the tyrant, that, meaning to revenge himself upon
Dion, who made war against him, he caused his son, whom
he had in his power, to be brought up in riot and wantonness.
This labour many save their enemies and do it themselves,
and so prove miserable parents of dissolute children. It was
an odious thing in the Israelites to sacrifice to devils their
sons and daughters which they had borne unto God, and
whom he avowed for his children, Ezek. xvi. 20; which, in a
spiritual sense, we certainly do, if we either neglect instructing them, or praying to God for them, or walking ex-

emplarily, as we ought, before them, or correcting them duly, or any other such means, as by which the seeds of grace may grow and prosper in them. And let us remember, that as brutes bring forth in their kind, and all parents their children; so we, being in the Lord's covenant of grace, bring forth, as by nature ours, so by the supernatural covenant and grace, his children also; and that he trusts us with the bringing them up for him, and in his nurture and instruction, Eph. vi. 4; which is a great matter, and wherein we must deal faithfully with him; that so under his blessing, we may fit them for his heavenly inheritance, provided for them with us. It is a during fruit of God's gracious covenant, when good parents by their godly care have gracious children; and that by which our faith is much confirmed.

Children, in their first days, have the greater benefit of good mothers, not only because they suck their milk, but in a sort, their manners also, by being continually with them, and receiving their first impressions from them. But afterwards, when they come to riper years, good fathers are more behoveful for their forming in virtue and good manners, by their greater wisdom and authority: and ofttimes also, by correcting the fruits of their mother's indulgence, by their severity.[2]

They are a blessing great, but dangerous. They come into the world at first with danger, both in respect of themselves, as passing sometimes, from the womb to the grave; sometimes, being born deformed in body; sometimes, incapable of understanding: as also in regard of the mother, the first day of their being in the world, being often her last in it. After their coming into the world through so many dangers, they come even into a world of dangers. In their infancy, how soon is the tender bud nipped, or bruised by sickness or otherwise! In their venturesome days, into how many needless dangers do they throw themselves, in which many perish, besides those into which God brings them, and that all their life long! Above all other, how great and many are their spiritual dan-

---

[2]Aristotle.

gers, both for nourishing and increasing the corruption which they bring into the world with them; and for diverting them from all goodness, which God's grace, and men's endeavour might work in them! These dangers and difficulties, howsoever they make not God's blessings in giving children to be no blessings, or deserving to be lightly esteemed; yet should they moderate our desire of them, and grief for their want: that none should say either to God or one to another, as Rachel did to Jacob, "Give me children, or else I die," Gen. xxx. 1: specially if we weigh withal, that though the Lord gives us divers towardly, and good; yet one or two proving lewd and wicked will break our tender hearts, more than all the rest will comfort us: like as in the natural body there is more grief by the aching of some one part, though but a tooth, than comfort and ease in the good and sound state of all the rest. If children considered aright of the careful thoughts, sorrows and fears, and sore pains withal of their parents, they would think they owed them more honour, service and obedience, than, for the most part, they do. We seldom consider and prize worthily the cares and pains of parents, till we become parents ourselves, and learn them by experience.

Many bodily diseases are hereditary; and so are many spiritual, in a sort; and that both by natural inclination, and moral imitation much more: that, as the Lord saith of Israel, "Thou art thy mother's daughter," Ezek. xvi. 45, so may it be said of many, that they are their fathers' and mothers' sons and daughters in evil. Yet, if it so come to pass, that God vouchsafe grace to the child of a wicked father, and that he see the sins which he hath done, he commonly hates them more vehemently, than if they had been in a stranger; and good reason, considering how they have been his dearest parent's ruin. Yea further, even where grace is wanting, the child, ofttimes, by observing and sometimes by feeling also the evil of his father's sin, is driven, though not from his evil way into a good way, yet into the contrary evil. Thus a covetous father often makes a prodigal son; so doth a prodigal a covetous. The son of the covetous taking knowledge how

odious his father's covetousness is to all; and therewith per-
suading himself, and being persuaded by others about him,
that there is enough, and more than enough for him, takes
occasion as prodigally to pour out, as his father hath miserly
hoarded up: as on the contrary, the son of the prodigal both
seeing, and feeling the hurt of his parent's lavishness, is
thereby provoked to lay the harder about him, for the repair-
ing of his father's ruins.

Love rather descends, than ascends; as streams of water
do; and no marvel, if men love where they live, as parents do
in children, and not they in them. Hence also is it, that
grandfathers are more affectionate towards their children's
children, than to their immediates, as seeing themselves further propagated in them, and by their means proceeding on to
a further degree of eternity, which all desire naturally, if not
in themselves, yet in their posterity. And hence it is, that
children brought up with their grandfathers, or grandmothers,
seldom do well, but are usually corrupted by their too great
indulgence.

It is much controverted, whether it be better, in the general, to bring up children under the severity of discipline, and
the rod, or no. And the wisdom of the flesh out of love to its
own, alleges many reasons to the contrary. But say men what
they will, or can, the wisdom of God is best; and that saith,
that "foolishness is bound up in the heart of a child, which the
rod of correction must drive out:" and that "he, who spares
his rod, hurts his son," Prov. xxii. 15; xiii. 24; not in the
affection of person, but effect of thing. And surely there is in
all children, though not alike, a stubbornness, and stoutness
of mind arising from natural pride, which must, in the first
place, be broken and beaten down; that so the foundation of
their education being laid in humility and tractableness, other
virtues may, in their time, be built thereon. This fruit of
natural corruption and root of actual rebellion both against
God and man must be destroyed, and no manner of way
nourished, except we will plant a nursery of contempt of
all good persons and things, and of obstinacy therein. It is

commendable in a horse, that he be stout and stomachful, being never to be left to his own government, but always to have his rider on his back, and the bit in his mouth. But who would have his child like his horse in his brutishness? Indeed such as are of great stomach, being thoroughly broken, and informed, become very serviceable,[3] for great designs: else, of horses they become asses, or worse: as Themistocles' master told him, when he was a child, that either he would bring some great good, or some great hurt to the commonwealth.[4] Neither is there need to fear, lest by this breaking, the children of great men should prove base-spirited and abject, and so unapt to great employments: for being Adam's sons, whose desire was to have been like unto God, and having those advantages for masterfulness and high thoughts, which great men's children want not, unto whom great affairs are appropriated usually, they will not easily be found unfurnished of stomach and stoutness of mind more than enough; wherein a little is dangerous, specially for making them unmeet for Christ's yoke, and to learn of him, who was lowly, and meek. Matt. xi. 29.

For the beating, and keeping down of this stubbornness parents must provide carefully for two things: first that children's wills and wilfulness be restrained and repressed, and that, in time; lest sooner than they imagine, the tender sprigs grow to that stiffness, that they will rather break than bow. Children should not know, if it could be kept from them, that they have a will in their own, but in their parents' keeping: neither should these words be heard from them, save by way of consent, "I will" or "I will not." And, if will be suffered at first to sway in them in small and lawful things, they will hardly after be restrained in great and ill matters, which their partial conceit, and inexperienced youth, with the lusts thereof and desire of liberty, shall deem small and lawful, as the former. And though good education, specially the grace of

[3]Erasmus.
[4]Plutarch.

God, may afterwards purge out much other evil and weaken this also: yet will such unbroken youth most commonly draw after it great disquietness in crosses, when they fall; and in the whole course of life, a kind of unwieldiness, inflexibility and obstinacy, prejudicial to the parties themselves and uncomfortable, at least, to such as converse with them. The second help is an inuring of them from the first, to such a meanness in all things, as may rather pluck them down, than lift them up: as by plain, and homely diet, and apparel; sending them to school betimes; and bestowing them afterwards, as they are fit, in some course of life, in which they may be exercised diligently, and the same rather under than above their estate: by not abetting them one against another, nor against any, specially before their faces, without great cause: nor by making them men and women, before they become good boys and girls. How oft have I observed, that parents, who have neither failed in diligent instructing of their children, nor in giving them good example, nor in correcting them duly, have only by straining too high this way, either endangered, or utterly overthrown their posterity! hereby lifting them up in their vain hearts, and teaching them to despise both mean things and persons; and themselves also, many times, amongst others: thereby drowning them, Icarus like, in a sea of mischief and misery, by their flying too high a pitch. And this must be the more minded, because there is in men an inbred desire, and that inordinate usually, to hoist up their children, as high, as may be: so as they half think they do them wrong, if they set them not higher, or as high, at least, as themselves, almost whether God will or not. Yea what place affords not some such, as make themselves their children's slaves, not caring how basely they themselves grovel in the earth, so they may set them on their tiptoes.

But first of all for children's competent education, specially for their disposing in some particular course, on which all are to settle at last, though some liberty of stepping this way, or that be given them for a while; as a man, though for his

pleasure he see many places, yet seeks his abode in some one
in the end,[5] there is required in their parents a thorough
discerning and right judgment of their disposition; which is as
difficult, as necessary. The difficulty ariseth from the partiality of parents towards their own: for that as the crow thinks
her own bird fairest, so do they commonly their children
towardly, and better than they are, or than any other
indifferent judge doth. This partiality in many is so gross, as
they not only deem small good things in them, great, and
great evils, small; but often account the same things well
becoming them and commendable, which in others they
would censure as indecent, and, it may be, enormous. This
pernicious error ariseth from self-love. For, as in nature, the
object cannot be seen, which is either too near the eye, or too
far from it; so neither can the disposition of that child be
rightly discerned, which lieth too near his father's heart. And
yet is the knowledge of this, so necessary, that we build not
either upon a vain, or uncertain foundation, with great hazard
of loss, both of labour, and expense, in sorting our child to his
particular calling and course of life; as all without it, is but a
very rash adventure. For as none are fit for every course, nor
hardly any for many, in any great degree, so every one is fit
for one or other: to which if his ability, and disposition be
applied, with any convenient diligence on his part and helps
by others; he may easily come to a mediocrity therein, if not
to some rareness. Hence was it, that fathers in some places,
used to lead their children to the shops of all kind of artificers,
to try how they could both handle their tools, and like their
works; that so they might bestow them accordingly. Some
wise men also have wished, that there might be established,
by public authority, a course for the due trial, and choice of
wits for several sciences. And surely, where there goes not
before a natural aptness and moral disposition also for some
calling; there will follow nothing but loss: loss of time, loss of
labour, loss of charges, and all; as when the seed is cast into

---

[5]Plutarch.

the barren ground. And as the midwife how skilful soever in
her art, cannot make the woman to be delivered, that was not
first with child; so neither can the best masters make their
scholars, or servants, to bring forth sciences, unless they have
an aptness thereunto first conceived in their brains.[6]

There is running in the breasts of most parents a strong
stream of partial affection towards some one, or other of their
children, above the rest, either for its beauty or wit or likeness to themselves, or some other fancied good in it; which is
always dangerous, and oft hurtful. Sometimes the Lord takes
away such before the rest, to punish the father's fondness:
and most commonly such if surviving, prove the worst of all
the rest, as growing hereby proud, and arrogant in themselves, presumptuous upon their father's love, and con-
temptuous of the rest of their brethren, and sisters; as we may
see in Esau, Absalom, and Adonijah, their fathers' darlings;
and in many more, in our daily experience. And though they
in themselves, which they seldom are free from, be not corrupted with pride; yet will the rest seldom, or never escape
the infection of envy at it; as is to be seen in Joseph's
brethren. It is natural for parents tenderly to love all their
children; and best for them to be as equal towards all, as may
be; reserving the bestowing of their best and greatest love, till
they see, where God bestows his. And if so be they cannot,
or will not command their inordinate affections, as they
should, yet it is wisdom to conceal them from their children,
whom else they may hurt so many ways; as the ape is said,
many times to kill her young ones by too strait embracing
them.

The Lord promises and affords long life to such as "honour
father and mother," Exod. xx. 12; whose days if he shorten
in this life for their good, he lengthens out with immortality in
glory. On the other side, he cuts off from the earth stubborn
and disobedient children suddenly and in sundry ways.[7] And

[6]Plato.
[7]Calvin.

if he give them long life, it is for a curse unto them. They also often die without children themselves; and if not, their children oftener pay them that which is due, and owing them from their parents. The history is note-worthy of the father, who being drawn by his son to the threshold of the house, by the hair of the head; cried to him, to draw him no further, for that he had drawn his father no further.[8] And how should they expect honour from their children who have dishonoured their parents? or a happy life, who despise the author of their life under God? This honour is due not only to them by whom we have our being; but to them also by whom our well-being is furthered.

2. John Locke:
Some Thoughts Concerning Education (1690)

John Locke (1632–1704) wrote one of the most comprehensive treatises on child rearing and education published in England prior to the 19th century. Throughout the 18th century, however, it was available to Americans only in editions printed in England. As a result, it is improbable that it was widely read in the colonies, since it was accessible only to the relatively few men educated in the colleges and to those who collected private libraries. Nonetheless, Locke's treatise must be read in conjunction with other English and American sources on child rearing and education, since its fundamental assumptions and prescriptions for practice are strikingly similar, in many respects, to those advocated by others who were writing quite independently of Locke.

Locke, the son of a Puritan family, was raised during the bitter religious and political controversies of the 1630's and 1640's which culminated in civil war in England. It is scarcely surprising, therefore, that many of the fundamental assumptions shaping his views on childhood mirrored those of others raised within the Puritan tradition.

---

[8]Melancthon.

When reading Locke, one must ask what assumptions he made about human nature and, more particularly, about the natures of infants and children. What forms of behavior were desired and sought? What role did Locke envisage for parents in the upbringing of their offspring, and what methods of child rearing did he advocate? What assumptions did he make about the functioning of the will, and to what degree did he wish to shape and control of the wills of children? What were the implications of these particular methods for the formation of personalities and the characteristics of adult behavior?

§ 30. And thus I have done with what concerns the body and health, which reduces itself to these few and easily observable rules. Plenty of open air, exercise, and sleep; plain diet, no wine or strong drink, and very little or no physic; not too warm and streight cloathing; especially the head and feet kept cold, and the feet often used to cold water and exposed to wet.

§ 31. Due care being to keep the body in strength and vigour, so that it may be able to obey and execute the orders of the mind; the next and principal business is, to set the mind right, that on all occasions it may be disposed to consent to nothing, but what may be suitable to the dignity and excellency of a rational creature.

§ 32. If what I have said in the beginning of this discourse be true, as I do not doubt but it is, viz. that the difference to be found in the manners and abilities of men, is owing more to their education than to any thing else; we have reason to conclude, that great care is to be had of the forming children's minds, and giving them that seasoning early, which shall influence their lives always after. For when they do well or ill, the praise or blame will be laid there: and when any thing is done awkwardly, the common saying will pass upon them, that it is suitable to their breeding.

§ 33. As the strength of the body lies chiefly in being able to endure hardships, so also does that of the mind. And the

From John Locke, "Some Thoughts concerning Education," (1690) in *The Works of John Locke, in Nine Volumes.* (9th ed.; London, 1794), Vol. VIII, pp. 26–43, 93–97, 102–4.

great principle and foundation of all virtue and worth is placed in this, that a man is able to deny himself his own desires, cross his own inclinations, and purely follow what reason directs as best, though the appetite lean the other way.

§ 34. The great mistake I have observed in people's breeding their children has been, that this has not been taken care enough of in its due season: that the mind has not been made obedient to discipline, and pliant to reason, when at first it was most tender, most easy to be bowed. Parents being wisely ordained by nature to love their children, are very apt, if reason watch not that natural affection very warily; are apt, I say, to let it run into fondness. They love their little ones, and it is their duty: but they often with them cherish their faults too. They must not be crossed, forsooth; they must be permitted to have their wills in all things; and they being in their infancies not capable of great vices, their parents think they may safely enough indulge their little irregularities, and make themselves sport with that pretty perverseness, which they think well enough becomes that innocent age. But to a fond parent, that would not have his child corrected for a perverse trick, but excused it, saying it was a small matter; Solon very well replied, "Aye, but custom is a great one."

§ 35. The fondling must be taught to strike, and call names; must have what he cries for, and do what he pleases. Thus parents, by humouring and cockering them when little, corrupt the principles of nature in their children, and wonder afterwards to taste the bitter waters, when they themselves have poisoned the fountain. For when their children are grown up, and these ill habits with them; when they are now too big to be dandled, and their parents can no longer make use of them as playthings; then they complain, that the brats are untoward and perverse; then they are offended to see them wilful, and are troubled with those ill humours, which they themselves infused and fomented in them; and then, perhaps too late, would be glad to get out those weeds which their own hands have planted, and which now have taken too deep root to be easily extirpated. For he that has been used to have his will in every thing, as long as he was in coats, why should we think it strange that he should desire it, and contend for it still, when he is in breeches? Indeed, as he grows more towards a man, age shows his faults the more, so that there be few parents then so blind, as not to see them! few so insensible as not to feel the ill effects of their own indulgence. He had the will of his maid before he could speak or go; he had the mastery of his parents ever since he could prattle; and why, now he is grown up, is stronger and wiser than he was then, why now of a sudden must he be restrained and curbed? Why must he at seven, fourteen, or twenty years old, lose the privilege which the parent's indulgence, till then, so largely allowed him? Try it in a dog, or an horse, or any other creature, and see whether the ill and resty tricks they have learned when young, are easily to be mended when they are knit: and yet none of those creatures are half so wilful and proud, or half so desirous to be masters of themselves and others, as man.

§ 36. We are generally wise enough to begin with them, when they are very young; and discipline betimes those other creatures we would make useful and good for somewhat. They are only our own offspring, that we neglect at this point; and having made them ill children, we foolishly expect they should be good men. For if the child must have grapes, or sugar-plums, when he has a mind to them, rather than make the poor baby cry, or be out of humour; why, when he is grown up, must he not be satisfied too, if his desires carry him to wine or women? They are objects as suitable to the longing of twenty-one or more years, as what he cried for, when little, was to the inclinations of a child. The having desires accommodated to the apprehensions and relish of those several ages, is not the fault, but the not having them subject to the rules and restraints of reason: the difference lies not in the having or not having appetites, but in the power to govern, and deny ourselves in them. He that is not used to submit his will to the reason of others, when he is young, will scarce hearken or submit to his own reason, when he is of an age to make use of it. And what kind of a man such a one is like to prove, is easy to foresee.

§ 37. These are oversights usually committed by those who seem to take the greatest care of their children's education. But, if we look into the common management of children, we shall have reason to wonder, in the great dissoluteness of manners, which the world complains of, that there are any footsteps at all left to virtue. I desire to know what vice can be named, which parents, and those about children, do not season them with, and drop into them the seeds of, as often as they are capable to receive them? I do not mean by the examples they give, and the patterns they set before them, which is encouragement enough; but that which I would take notice of here, is the downright teaching them vice, and actual putting them out of the way of virtue. Before they can go, they principle them with violence, revenge, and cruelty. "Give me a blow that I may beat him," is a lesson which most children every day hear: and it is thought nothing, because their hands have not strength enough to do any mischief. But I ask, does not this corrupt their minds? is not this the way of force and violence, that they are set in? and if they have been taught when little, to strike and hurt others by proxy, and encouraged to rejoice in the harm they have brought upon them, and see them suffer; are they not pre-pared to do it, when they are strong enough to be felt them-selves, and can strike to some purpose?

The coverings of our bodies, which are for modesty, warmth, and defence, are, by the folly or vice of parents, recommended to their children for other uses. They are made matter of vanity and emulation. A child is set a longing after a new suit, for the finery of it: and when the little girl is tricked up in her new gown and commode, how can her mother do less than teach her to admire herself, by calling her, "her little queen," and "her princess?" Thus the little ones are taught to be proud of their cloaths, before they can put them on. And why should they not continue to value themselves for this outside fashionableness of the taylor or tire-woman's making, when their parents have so early instructed them to do so?

Lying and equivocations, and excuses little different from lying, are put into the mouths of young people, and commended in apprentices and children, whilst they are for their master's or parent's advantage. And can it be thought that he, that finds the straining of truth dispensed with, and encouraged, whilst it is for his godly master's turn, will not make use of that privilege for himself, when it may be for his own profit?

Those of the meaner sort are hindered by the streightness of their fortunes, from encouraging intemperance in their children, by the temptation of their diet, or invitations to eat or drink more than enough: but their own ill examples, whenever plenty comes in their way, show that it is not the dislike of drunkenness and gluttony that keeps them from excess, but want of materials. But if we look into the houses of those who are a little warmer in their fortunes, there eating and drinking are made so much the great business and happiness of life, that children are thought neglected, if they have not their share of it. Sauces, and ragouts, and foods disguised by all the arts of cookery, must tempt their palates, when their bellies are full: and then, for fear the stomach should be overcharged, a pretence is found for the other glass of wine, to help digestion, though it only serves to increase the surfeit.

Is my young master a little out of order? the first question is, "What will my dear eat? what shall I get for thee?" Eating and drinking are instantly pressed; and every body's invention is set on work to find out something luscious and delicate enough to prevail over that want of appetite, which nature has wisely ordered in the beginning of distempers, as a defence against their increase; that, being freed from ordinary labour of digesting any new load in the stomach, she may be at leisure to correct and master the peccant humours.

And where children are so happy in the care of their parents, as by their prudence to be kept from the excess of their tables, to the sobriety of a plain and simple diet; yet there too they are scarce to be preserved from the contagion that poisons the mind. Though by a discreet management, whilst they are under tuition, their healths, perhaps, may be pretty well secured; yet their desires must need yield to the lessons, which everywhere will be read to them upon this part of epicurism. The commendation that eating well has every-where, cannot fail to be a successful incentive to natural appetite, and bring them quickly to the liking and expence of a fashionable table. This shall have from every one, even the reprovers of vice, the title of living well. And what shall sullen reason dare to say against the public testimony? or can it hope to be heard, if it should call that luxury, which is so much owned, and universally practised by those of the best quality?

This is now so grown a vice, and has so great supports, that I know not whether it do not put in for the name of virtue; and whether it will not be thought folly, or want of knowledge of the world, to open one's mouth against it. And truly I should suspect, that what I have here said of it might be censured, as a little satire out of my way, did I not mention it with this view, that it might awaken the care and watchfulness of parents in the education of their children; when they see how they are beset on every side, not only with temptations, but instructors to vice, and that perhaps in those they thought places of security.

I shall not dwell any longer on this subject; much less run over all the particulars, that would show what pains are used to corrupt children, and instil principles of vice into them: but I desire parents soberly to consider, what irregularity or vice there is, which children are not visibly taught; and whether it be not their duty and wisdom to provide them other instructions.

§ 38. It seems plain to me, that the principle of all virtue and excellency lies in a power of denying ourselves the satisfaction of our own desires, where reason does not authorise them. This power is to be got and improved by custom, made easy and familiar by an early practice. If therefore I might be heard, I would advise, that, contrary to the ordinary way, children should be used to submit to their desires, and go without their longings, even from their very cradles. The very first thing they should learn to know, should be, that they were not to have any thing, because it pleased them, but because it was thought fit for them. If things suitable to their wants were supplied to them, so that they were never suffered to have what they once cried for, they would learn to be content without it; would never with bawling and peevishness contend for mastery; nor be half so uneasy to themselves and others as they are, because from the first beginning they are not thus handled. If they were never suffered to obtain their desire by the impatience they expressed for it, they would no more cry for other things, than they do for the moon.

§ 39. I say not this, as if children were not to be indulged in any thing, or that I expected they should, in hanging-sleeves, have the reason and conduct of counsellors. I consider them as children, who must be tenderly used, who must play, and have play-things. That which I mean is, that whenever they craved what was not fit for them to have, or do, they should not be permitted it, because they were little and desired it: nay, whatever they were importunate for, they should be sure, for that very reason, to be denied. I have seen children at a table, who, whatever was there, never asked for any thing, but contentedly took what was given them: and at another place I have seen others cry for every thing they saw, must be served out of every dish, and that first too. What made this vast difference but this, that one was accustomed to have what they called or cried for, the other to go without it? The younger they are, the less, I think, are their unruly and disorderly appetites to be complied with: and the less reason they have of their own, the more are they to be under the absolute power and restraint of those, in whose hands they are. From which I confess, it will follow, that none but discreet people should be about them. If the world commonly does otherwise, I cannot help that. I am saying what I think should be; which, if it were already in fashion, I should not need to trouble the world with a discourse on this subject. But yet I doubt not but, when it is considered, there will be others of opinion with me, that the sooner this way is begun with children, the easier it will be for them, and their governors too: and that this ought to be observed as an inviolable maxim, that whatever once is denied them, they are certainly not to obtain by crying or importunity; unless one has a mind to teach them to be impatient and troublesome, by rewarding them for it, when they are so.

§ 40. Those therefore that intend ever to govern their children, should begin it whilst they are very little; and look that they perfectly comply with the will of their parents. Would you have your son obedient to you, when past a child? Be sure then to establish the authority of a father, as soon as he is capable of submission, and can understand in whose power he is. If you would have him stand in awe of you, imprint it in his infancy; and, as he approaches more to a man, admit him nearer to your familiarity: so shall you have him your obedient subject (as is fit) whilst he is a child, and your affectionate friend when he is a man. For methinks they mightily misplace the treatment due to their children, who are indulgent and familiar when they are little, but severe to them, and keep them at a distance when they are grown up. For liberty and indulgence can do no good to children: their want of judgment makes them stand in need of restraint and discipline. And, on the contrary, imperiousness and severity is but an ill way of treating men, who have reason of their own to guide them, unless you have a mind to make your children, when grown up, weary of you; and secretly to say within themselves, "When will you die, father?"

§ 41. I imagine every one will judge it reasonable, that their children, when little, should look upon their parents as their lords, their absolute governors; and, as such, stand in awe of them: and that, when they come to riper years, they should look on them as their best, as their only sure friends: and, as such, love and reverence them. The way I have mentioned, if I mistake not, is the only one to obtain this. We must look upon our children, when grown up, to be like ourselves; with the same passions, the same desires. We would be thought rational creatures, and have our freedom; we love not to be uneasy under constant rebukes and brow-beatings; nor can we bear severe humours, and great distance, in those we converse with. Whoever has such treatment when he is a man, will look out other company, other friends, other conversation, with whom he can be at ease. If therefore a strict hand be kept over children from the beginning, they will in that age be tractable, and quietly submit to it, as never having known any other: and if, as they grow up to the use of reason, the rigour of government be, as they deserve it, gently relaxed, the father's brow more smoothed to them, and the distance by degrees abated: his former restraints will increase their love, when they find it was only a kindness for them, and a care to make them capable to deserve the favour of their parents, and the esteem of every body else.

§ 42. Thus much for the settling your authority over children in general. Fear and awe ought to give you the first power over their minds, and love and friendship in riper years to hold it: for the time must come, when they will be past the rod and correction; and then, if the love of you make them not obedient and dutiful; if the love of virtue and reputation keep them not in laudable courses; I ask, what hold will you have upon them, to turn them to it? Indeed, fear of having a scanty portion, if they displease you, may make them slaves to your estate; but they will be never the less ill and wicked in private, and that restraint will not last always. Every man must some time or other be trusted to himself, and his own conduct; and he that is a good, a virtuous, and able man, must be made so within. And therefore, what he is to receive from education, what is to sway and influence his life, must be something put into him betimes: habits woven into the very principles of his nature; and not a counterfeit carriage, and dissembled outside, put on by fear, only to avoid the present anger of a father, who perhaps may disinherit him.

§ 43. This being laid down in general, as the course ought

to be taken, it is fit we come now to consider the parts of the discipline to be used, a little more particularly. I have spoken so much of carrying a strict hand over children, that perhaps I shall be suspected of not considering enough what is due to their tender age and constitutions. But that opinion will vanish, when you have heard me a little farther. For I am very apt to think, that great severity of punishment does but very little good; nay, great harm in education: and I believe it will be found, that, cæteris paribus, those children who have been most chastised, seldom make the best men. All that I have hitherto contended for, is, that whatsoever rigour is necessary, it is more to be used, the younger children are; and, having by a due application wrought its effect, it is to be relaxed, and changed into a milder sort of government.

§ 44. A compliance, and suppleness of their wills, being by a steady hand introduced by parents, before children have memories to retain the beginnings of it, will seem natural to them, and work afterwards in them, as if it were so; preventing all occasions of struggling, or repining. The only care is, that it be begun early, and inflexibly kept to, till awe and respect be grown familiar, and there appears not the least reluctancy in the submission, and ready obedience of their minds. When this reverence is once thus established, (which it must be early, or else it will cost pains and blows to recover it, and the more, the longer it is deferred) it is by it, mixed still with as much indulgence, as they made not an ill use of, and not by beating, chiding, or other servile punishments, they are for the future to be governed, as they grow up to more understanding.

§ 45. That this is so, will be easily allowed, when it is but considered what is to be aimed at, in an ingenuous education; and upon what it turns.

1. He that has not a mastery over his inclinations, he that knows not how to resist the importunity of present pleasure or pain, for the sake of what reason tells him is fit to be done, wants the true principle of virtue and industry; and is in danger of never being good for any thing. This temper, there-

fore, so contrary to unguided nature, is to be got betimes; and this habit, as the true foundation of future ability and happiness, is to be wrought into the mind, as early as may be, even from the first dawnings of any knowledge or apprehension in children; and so to be confirmed in them, by all the care and ways imaginable, by those who have the oversight of their education.

§ 46.   2. On the other side, if the mind be curbed, and humbled too much in children; if their spirits be abased and broken much, by too strict an hand over them; they lose all their vigour and industry, and are in a worse state than the former. For extravagant young fellows, that have liveliness and spirit, come sometimes to be set right, and so make able and great men: but dejected minds, timorous and tame, and low spirits, are hardly ever to be raised, and very seldom attain to any thing. To avoid the danger that is on either hand is the great art: and he that has found a way how to keep up a child's spirit, easy, active, and free; and yet, at the same time, to restrain him from many things he has a mind to, and to draw him to things that are uneasy to him; he, I say, that knows how to reconcile these seeming contradictions, has, in my opinion, got the true secret of education.

§ 47. The usual lazy and short way by chastisement, and the rod, which is the only instrument of government that tutors generally know, or ever think of, is the most unfit of any to be used in education; because it tends to both those mischiefs; which, as we have shown, are the Scylla and Charybdis, which, on the one hand or the other, ruin all that miscarry.

§ 48.   1. This kind of punishment contributes not at all to the mastery of our natural propensity to indulge corporal and present pleasure, and to avoid pain at any rate; but rather encourages it; and thereby strengthens that in us, which is the root, from whence spring all vicious actions and the irregularities of life. From what other motive, but of sensual pleasure, and pain, does a child act, who drudges at his book against his inclination, or abstains from eating unwholesome fruit, that he takes pleasure in, only out of fear of whipping? He in this only prefers the greater corporal pleasure, or avoids the greater corporal pain. And what is it to govern his actions, and direct his conduct, by such motives as these? what is it, I say, but to cherish that principle in him, which it is our business to root out and destroy? And therefore I cannot think any correction useful to a child, where the shame of suffering for having done amiss does not work more upon him than the pain.

§ 49.   2. This sort of correction naturally breeds an aversion to that which is the tutor's business to create a liking to. How obvious is it to observe, that children come to hate things which were at first acceptable to them, when they find themselves whipped, and chid, and teazed about them? And it is not to be wondered at in them; when grown men would not be able to be reconciled to any thing by such ways. Who is there that would not be disgusted with any innocent recreation, in itself indifferent to him, if he should with blows, or ill language, be hauled to it, when he had no mind? or be constantly so treated, for some circumstances in his application to it? This is natural to be so. Offensive circumstances ordinarily infest innocent things, which they are joined with: and the very sight of a cup, wherein any one uses to take nauseous physic, turns his stomach; so that nothing will relish well out of it, though the cup be ever so clean, and well-shaped, and of the richest materials.

§ 50.   3. Such a sort of slavish discipline makes a slavish temper. The child submits, and dissembles obedience, whilst the fear of the rod hangs over him; but when that is removed, and, by being out of sight, he can promise himself impunity, he gives the greater scope to his natural inclination; which by this way is not at all altered, but on the contrary heightened and increased in him; and after such restraint, breaks out usually with the more violence. Or,

§ 51.   4. If severity carried to the highest pitch does prevail, and works a cure upon the present unruly distemper, it is often bringing in the room of it worse and more dangerous disease, by breaking the mind; and then, in the place of a disorderly young fellow, you have a low-spirited moped creature: who, however with his unnatural sobriety he may please silly people, who commend tame inactive children, because they make no noise, nor give them any trouble; yet, at last, will probably prove as uncomfortable a thing to his friends, as he will be, all his life, an useless thing to himself and others.

§ 52. Beating then, and all other sorts of slavish and corporal punishments, are not the discipline fit to be used in the education of those who would have wise, good, and ingenuous men; and therefore very rarely to be applied, and that only on great occasions, and cases of extremity. On the other side, to flatter children by rewards of things that are pleasant to them, is as carefully to be avoided. He that will give to his son apples, or sugar-plums, or what else of this kind he is most delighted with, to make him learn his book, does but authorise his love of pleasure, and cocker up that dangerous propensity, which he ought by all means to subdue and stifle in him. You can never hope to teach him to master it, whilst you compound for the check you give his inclination in one place, by the satisfaction you propose to it in another. To make a good, a wise, and a virtuous man, it is fit he should learn to cross his appetite, and deny his inclination to riches, finery, or pleasing his palate, &c. whenever his reason advises the contrary, and his duty requires it. But when you draw him to do any thing that is fit, by the offer of money; or reward the pains of learning his book, by the pleasure of a luscious morsel; when you promise him a lace-cravat, or a fine new suit, upon performance of some of his little tasks; what do you, by proposing these as rewards, but allow them to be the good things he should aim at, and thereby encourage his longing for them, and accustom him to place his happiness in them? Thus people, to prevail with children to be industrious about their grammar, dancing, or some other such matter, of no great moment to the happiness or usefulness of their lives, by misapplied rewards and punishments, sacrifice their virtue, invert the order of their education, and teach them luxury, pride, or covetousness, &c. For in this way, flattering those wrong inclinations, which they should restrain and suppress, they lay the foundations of those future vices, which cannot be avoided, but by curbing our desires, and accustoming them early to submit to reason.

§ 53. I say not this, that I would have children kept from the conveniencies or pleasures of life, that are not injurious to their health or virtue: on the contrary, I would have their lives made as pleasant, and as agreeable to them as may be, in a plentiful enjoyment of whatsoever might innocently delight them: provided it be with this caution, that they have these enjoyments, only as the consequences of the state of esteem and acceptation they are in with their parents and governors; but they should never be offered or bestowed on them, as the reward of this or that particular performance, that they show an aversion to, or to which they would not have applied themselves without that temptation.

§ 54. But if you take away the rod on one hand, and these little encouragements, which they are taken with, on the other; how then (will you say) shall children be governed? Remove hope and fear, and there is an end of all discipline. I grant, that good and evil, reward and punishment, are the only motives to a rational creature; these are the spur and reins, whereby all mankind are set on work and guided, and therefore they are to be made use of to children too. For I advise their parents and governors always to carry this in their minds, that children are to be treated as rational creatures.

§ 55. Rewards, I grant, and punishments must be proposed to children, if we intend to work upon them. The mistake, I imagine, is, that those that are generally made use of, are ill chosen. The pains and pleasures of the body are, I think, of ill consequence, when made the rewards and punishments whereby men would prevail on their children: for, as I said before, they serve but to increase and strengthen those inclinations, which it is our business to subdue and master. What principle of virtue do you lay in a child, if you will

redeem his desires of one pleasure by the proposal of another? This is but to enlarge his appetite, and instruct it to
wander. If a child cries for an unwholesome and dangerous
fruit, you purchase his quiet by giving him a less hurtful
sweet-meat. This perhaps may preserve his health, but spoils
his mind, and sets that farther out of order. For here you only
change the object; but flatter still his appetite, and allow that
must be satisfied, wherein, as I have showed, lies the root of
the mischief: and till you bring him to be able to bear a denial
of that satisfaction, the child may at present be quiet and
orderly, but the disease is not cured. By this way of proceeding you foment and cherish in him that which is the spring,
from whence all the evil flows; which will be sure on the next
occasion to break out again with more violence, give him
stronger longings, and you more trouble.

§ 56. The rewards and punishments then whereby we
should keep children in order, are quite of another kind; and
of that force, that when we can get them once to work, the
business, I think, is done, and the difficulty is over. Esteem
and disgrace are, of all others, the most powerful incentives
to the mind, when once it is brought to relish them. If you can
once get into children a love of credit, and an apprehension of
shame and disgrace, you have put into them the true principle, which will constantly work, and incline them to the
right. But it will be asked, How shall this be done?

I confess, it does not, at first appearance, want some
difficulty; but yet I think it worth our while to seek the ways
(and practise them when found) to attain this, which I look on
as the great secret of education.

§ 57. First, children (earlier perhaps than we think) are
very sensible of praise and commendation. They find a pleasure in being esteemed and valued, especially by their parents, and those whom they depend on. If therefore the father
caress and commend them, when they do well; show a cold
and neglectful countenance to them upon doing ill; and this
accompanied by a like carriage of the mother, and all others
that are about them; it will in a little time make them sensible

of the difference: and this, if constantly observed, I doubt not
but will of itself work more than threats or blows, which lose
their force, when once grown common, and are of no use
when shame does not attend them: and therefore are to be
forborn, and never to be used, but in the case here-
after-mentioned, when it is brought to extremity.

§ 58. But, secondly, to make the sense of esteem or disgrace sink the deeper, and be of the more weight, other
agreeable or disagreeable things should constantly accompany these different states; not as particular rewards and
punishments of this or that particular action, but as necessarily belonging to, and constantly attending one, who by his
carriage has brought himself into a state of disgrace or commendation. By which way of treating them, children may as
much as possible be brought to conceive, that those that are
commended and in esteem for doing well, will necessarily be
beloved and cherished by every body, and have all other good
things as a consequence of it; and, on the other side, when
any one by miscarriage falls into dis-esteem, and cares not to
preserve his credit, he will unavoidably fall under neglect and
contempt: and, in that state, the want of whatever might
satisfy or delight him, will follow. In this way the objects of
their desires are made assisting to virtue; when a settled
experience from the beginning teaches children, that the
things they delight in, belong to, and are to be enjoyed by
those only, who are in a state of reputation. If by these means
you can come once to shame them out of their faults, (for
besides that, I would willingly have no punishment) and make
them love with the pleasure of being well thought on, you
may turn them as you please, and they will be in love with all
the ways of virtue.

§ 59. The great difficulty here is, I imagine, from the folly
and perverseness of servants, who are hardly to be hindered
from crossing herein the design of the father and mother.
Children discountenanced by their parents for any fault, find
usually a refuge and relief in the caresses of those foolish
flatterers, who thereby undo whatever the parents endeavour

to establish. When the father or mother looks sour on the child, every body else should put on the same coldness to him, and no-body give him countenance, till forgiveness asked, and a reformation of his fault, has set him right again, and restored him to his former credit. If this were constantly observed, I guess there would be little need of blows or chiding: their own case and satisfaction would quickly teach children to court commendation, and avoid doing that, which they found every body condemned, and they were sure to suffer for, without being chid or beaten. This would teach them modesty and shame; and they would quickly come to have a natural abhorrence for that, which they found made them slighted and neglected by every body. But how this inconvenience from servants is to be remedied, I must leave to parents care and consideration. Only I think it of great importance; and that they are very happy, who can get discreet people about their children.

§ 60. Frequent beating or chiding is therefore carefully to be avoided; because this sort of correction never produces any good, farther than it serves to raise shame and abhorrence of the miscarriage that brought it on them. And if the greatest part of the trouble be not the sense that they have done amiss, and the apprehension that they have drawn on themselves the just displeasure of their best friends, the pain of whipping will work but an imperfect cure. It only patches up for the present, and skins it over, but reaches not to the bottom of the sore. Ingenuous shame, and the apprehension of displeasure, are the only true restraints: these alone ought to hold the reins, and keep the child in order. But corporal punishments must necessarily lose that effect, and wear out the sense of shame, where they frequently return. Shame in children has the same place that modesty has in women; which cannot be kept, and often transgressed against. And as to the apprehension of displeasure in the parents, they will come to be very insignificant, if the marks of that displeasure quickly cease, and a few blows fully expiate. Parents should well consider, what faults in their children are weighty enough to deserve the declaration of their anger: but when their displeasure is once declared to a degree that carries any punishment with it, they ought not presently to lay by the severity of their brows, but to restore their children to their former grace with some difficulty; and delay a full reconciliation, till their conformity, and more than ordinary merit, make good their amendment. If this be not so ordered, punishment will by familiarity become a mere thing of course, and lose all its influence: offending, being chastised, and then forgiven, will be thought as natural and necessary as noon, night, and morning, following one another.

• • • • •

§ 103. I told you before, that children love liberty; and therefore they should be brought to do the things that are fit for them, without feeling any restraint laid upon them. I now tell you, they love something more: and that is dominion: and this is the first original of most vicious habits, that are ordinary and natural. This love of power and dominion shows itself very early, and that in these two things.

§ 104. 1. We see children (as soon almost as they are born, I am sure long before they can speak) cry, grow peevish, sullen, and out of humour, for nothing but to have their wills. They would have their desires submitted to by others; they contend for a ready compliance from all about them, especially from those that stand near or beneath them in age or degree, as soon as they come to consider others with those distinctions.

§ 105.   2. Another thing, wherein they show their love of dominion, is their desire to have things to be theirs; they would have property and possession, pleasing themselves with the power which that seems to give, and the right they thereby have to dispose of them as they please. He that has not observed these two humours working very betimes in children has taken little notice of their actions: and he who thinks that those two roots of almost all the injustice and contention that so disturb human life, are not early to be weeded out, and contrary habits introduced, neglects the proper season to lay the foundations of a good and worthy man. To do this, I imagine, these following things may somewhat conduce.

§ 106.   1. That a child should never be suffered to have what he craves, much less what he cries for, I had said, or so much as speaks for. But that being apt to be misunderstood, and interpreted as if I meant a child should never speak to his parents for any thing, which will perhaps be thought to lay too great a curb on the minds of children, to the prejudice of that love and affection which should be between them and their parents; I shall explain myself a little more particularly. It is fit that they should have liberty to declare their wants to their parents, and that with all tenderness they should be hearkened to, and supplied, at least whilst they are very little. But it is one thing to say, I am hungry; another to say, I would have roast-meat. Having declared their wants, their natural wants, the pain they feel from hunger, thirst, cold, or any other necessity of nature, it is the duty of their parents, and those about them, to relieve them; but children must leave it to the choice and ordering of their parents what they think properest for them, and how much; and must not be permitted to choose for themselves; and say, I would have wine, or white-bread; the very naming of it should make them lose it.

§ 107. That which parents should take care of here, is to distinguish between the wants of fancy and those of nature; which Horace has well taught them to do in this verse,

Queis humana fibi doleat natura negatis.

Those are truly natural wants, which reason alone, without some other help, is not able to silence again, nor keep from disturbing us. The pains of sickness and hurts, hunger, thirst and cold, want of sleep and rest, or relaxation of the part wearied with labour, are what all men feel, and the best disposed mind cannot but be sensible of their uneasiness; and therefore ought, by fit applications, to seek their removal, though not with impatience, or over-great haste, upon the first approaches of them, where delay does not threaten some irreparable harm. The pains that come from the necessities of nature, are monitors to us to beware of greater mischiefs, which they are the forerunners of; and therefore they must not be wholly neglected, nor strained too far. But yet, the more children can be inured to hardships of this kind, by a wise care to make them stronger in body and mind, the better it will be for them. I need not here give any caution to keep within the bounds of doing them good, and to take care, that what children are made to suffer should neither break their spirits, nor injure their health; parents being but too apt of themselves to incline, more than they should, to the softer side.

But, whatever compliance the necessities of nature may require, the wants of fancy children should never be gratified in, nor suffered to mention, The very speaking for any such thing should make them lose it. Clothes, when they need, they must have; but if they speak for this stuff, or that colour, they should be sure to go without it. Not that I would have parents purposely cross the desires of their children in matters of indifferency: on the contrary, where their carriage deserves it, and one is sure it will not corrupt or effeminate their minds, and make them fond of trifles, I think, all things should be contrived, as much as could be, to their satisfaction, that they might find the ease and pleasure of doing well. The best for children is, that they should not place any pleasure in such things at all, nor regulate their delight by their fancies; but be indifferent to all that nature has made so. This is what their parents and teachers should chiefly aim at: but till this be obtained, all that I oppose here, is the liberty of asking; which, in these things of conceit, ought to be restrained by a constant forfeiture annexed to it.

This may perhaps be thought a little too severe, by the natural indulgence of tender parents: but yet it is no more then necessary. For since the method I propose is to banish the rod, this restraint of their tongues will be of great use to settle that awe we have elsewhere spoken of, and to keep up in them the respect and reverence due to their parents. Next, it will teach them to keep in, and so master their inclinations. By this means they will be brought to learn the art of stifling their desires, as soon as they rise up in them, when they are easiest to be subdued. For giving vent, gives life and strength to our appetites; and he that has the confidence to turn his wishes into demands, will be but a little way from thinking he ought to obtain them. This I am sure of, every one can more easily bear a denial from himself, than from any body else. They should therefore be accustomed betimes to consult and make use of their reason, before they give allowance to their inclinations. It is a great step towards the mastery of our desires, to give this stop to them, and shut them up in silence. This habit, got by children, of staying the forwardness of their fancies, and deliberating whether it be fit or no before they speak, will be of no small advantage to them in matters of greater consequence in the future course of their lives. For that which I cannot too often inculcate, it, that whatever the matter be, about which it is conversant, whether great or small, the main (I had almost said only) thing to be considered, in every action of a child, is, what influence it will have upon his mind; what habit it tends to, and is like to settle in him; how it will become him when he is bigger; and, if it be encouraged, whither it will lead him when he is grown up.

My meaning therefore is not, that children should purposely be made uneasy: this would relish too much of inhumanity and ill-nature, and be apt to infect them with it. They should be brought to deny their appetites: and their minds, as well as bodies, be made vigorous, easy and strong, by the custom of having their inclinations in subjection, and their bodies exercised with hardships; but all this without giving them any mark or apprehension of ill-will towards them. The constant loss of what they craved or carved to themselves should teach them modesty, submission, and a power to forbear: but the rewarding their modesty and silence, by giving them what they liked, should also assure them of the love of those who rigorously exacted this obedience. The contenting themselves now, in the want of what they wished for, is a virtue, that another time should be rewarded with what is suited and acceptable to them; which should be bestowed on them, as if it were a natural consequence of their good behavior, and not a bargain about it. But you will lose your labour, and, what is more, their love and reverence too, if they can receive from others what you deny them. This is to be kept very stanch, and carefully to be watched. And here the servants come again in my way.

· · · · ·

§ 111. Crying is a fault that should not be tolerated in children; not only for the unpleasant and unbecoming noise it fills the house with, but for more considerable reasons, in reference to the children themselves; which is to be our aim in education.

Their crying is of two sorts; either stubborn and domineering, or querulous and whining.

1. Their crying is very often a striving for mastery, and an open declaration of their insolence or obstinacy: when they have not the power to obtain their desire, they will, by their clamour and sobbing, maintain their title and right to it. This is an avowed continuing of their claim, and a sort of remonstrance against the oppression and injustice of those who deny them what they have a mind to.

§ 112.   2. Sometimes their crying is the effect of pain or true sorrow, and a bemoaning themselves under it.

These two, if carefully observed, may, by the mien, looks, and actions, and particularly by the tone of their crying, be easily distinguished; but neither of them must be suffered, much less encouraged.

1. The obstinate or stomachful crying should by no means be permitted; because it is but another way of flattering their desires, and encouraging those passions, which it is our main business to subdue: and if it be, as often it is, upon the receiving any correction, it quite defeats all the good effects

of it; for any chastisement, which leaves them in this declared opposition, only serves to make them worse. The restraints and punishments laid on children are all misapplied and lost, as far as they do not prevail over their wills, teach them to submit their passions, and make their minds supple and pliant to what their parents' reason advises them now, and so prepare them to obey what their own reason shall advise hereafter. But if, in any thing wherein they are crossed, they may be suffered to go away crying, they confirm themselves in their desires, and cherish the ill humour, with a declaration of their right, and a resolution to satisfy their inclinations the first opportunity. This therefore is another argument against the frequent use of blows: for, whenever you come to that extremity, it is not enough to whip or beat them; you must do it, till you find you have subdued their minds; till with submission and patience they yield to the correction; which you shall best discover by their crying, and their ceasing from it upon your bidding. Without this, the beating of children is but a passionate tyranny over them: and it is mere cruelty, and not correction, to put their bodies in pain, without doing their minds any good. As this gives us a reason why children should seldom be corrected, so it also prevents their being so. For if, whenever they are chastised, it were done thus without passion, soberly and yet effectually too, laying on the blows and smart, not furiously and all at once, but slowly, with reasoning between, and with observation how it wrought, stopping when it had made them pliant, penitent, and yielding; they would seldom need the like punishment again, being made careful to avoid the fault that deserved it. Besides, by this means, as the punishment would not be lost, for being too little, and not effectual: so it would be kept from being too much, if we gave off as soon as we perceived that it reached the mind, and that was bettered. For, since the chiding or beating of children should be always the least that possibly may be, that which is laid on in the heat of anger, seldom observes that measure; but is commonly more than should be, though it prove less than enough.

3. Cotton Mather:
On the Education of His Children (1706)

Cotton Mather (1663–1728) was born, raised, lived, and died in Boston, Massachusetts, where he became one of the outstanding ministers of New England. His father, the Reverend Increase Mather, served as President of Harvard College and as minister of the Second Congregational Church in Boston. Cotton Mather served as co-pastor with his father. Both in the pulpit and in print, he offered opinions and advice to the public on their religious and secular lives, including the rearing and education of their children.

In his private diary, Mather included a brief set of observations on the raising of his own children that succinctly defines the principles he believed himself to be practicing. To what extent did he share the assumptions and the goals of other English and American writers of the 17th and 18th centuries? And to what extent did he manage to implement his precepts in the daily experiences of his own children and family, as recorded in his diary?

1705/6; FEBRUARY

SOME SPECIAL POINTS, RELATING TO THE EDUCATION OF MY CHILDREN

I. I pour out continual Prayers and Cries to the God of all Grace for them, that He will be a Father to my Children, and bestow His Christ and His Grace upon them, and guide them with His Councils, and bring them to His Glory.

And in this Action, I mention them distinctly, every one by Name unto the Lord.

From Worthington Chauncey Ford (ed.), *Diary of Cotton Mather, 1681–1724*, Collections of the Massachusetts Historical Society, 7th Series, 2 vols. (Boston, 1911–12), Vol. I, pp. 534–37.

II. I begin betimes to entertain them with delightful Stories, especially *scriptural* ones. And still conclude with some *Lesson* of Piety; bidding them to learn that *Lesson* from the *Story*.

And thus, every Day at the *Table,* I have used myself to tell a *Story* before I rise; and make the *Story* useful to the *Olive Flants about the Table.*

III. When the Children at any time accidentally come in my way, it is my custome to lett fall some *Sentence* or other, that may be monitory and profitable to them.

This Matter proves to me, a Matter of some Study, and Labour, and Contrivance. But who can tell, what may be the Effect of a *continual Dropping?*

IV. I essay betimes, to engage the Children, in Exercises of Piety; and especially *secret Prayer,* for which I give them very plain and brief *Directions,* and suggest unto them the *Petitions,* which I would have them to make before the Lord, and which I therefore explain to their Apprehension and Capacity. And I often call upon them; *Child, Don't you forgett every Day, to go alone, and pray as I have directed you!*

V. Betimes I try to form in the Children a Temper of *Benignity.* I put them upon doing of Services and Kindnesses for one another, and for other Children. I applaud them, when I see them Delight in it. I upbraid all Aversion to it. I caution them exquisitely against all Revenges of Injuries. I instruct them, to return good Offices for evil Ones. I show them, how they will by this *Goodness* become like to the Good GOD, and His Glorious CHRIST. I lett them discern, that I am not satisfied, except when they have a Sweetness of Temper shining in them.

VI. As soon as tis possible, I make the Children learn to *write.* And when they can *write,* I employ them in Writing out the most agreeable and profitable Things, that I can invent for them. In this way, I propose to fraight their minds with *excellent Things,* and have a deep Impression made upon their Minds by such Things.

VII. I mightily endeavour it, that the Children may betimes, be acted by Principles of *Reason* and *Honour.*

I first begett in them an high Opinion of their Father's
Love to them, and of his being best able to judge, what shall
be good for them.

Then I make them sensible, tis a Folly for them to pretend
unto any Witt and Will of their own; they must resign all to
me, who will be sure to do what is best; my word must be
their Law.

I cause them to understand, that it is an *hurtful* and a
shameful thing to do amiss. I aggravate this, on all Occasions;
and lett them see how *amiable* they will render themselves by
well doing.

The *first Chastisement,* which I inflict for an ordinary
Fault, is, to lett the Child see and hear me in an Astonish-
ment, and hardly able to beleeve that the Child could do so
base a Thing, but beleeving that they will never do it again.

I would never come, to give a child a *Blow;* except in Case
of *Obstinacy;* or some gross Enormity.

To be chased for a while out of *my Presence,* I would make
to be look'd upon, as the sorest Punishment in the Family.

I would by all possible Insinuations gain this Point upon
them, that for them to learn all the brave Things in the world,
is the bravest Thing in the world. I am not fond of proposing
Play to them, as a Reward of any diligent Application to learn
what is good; lest they should think *Diversion* to be a better
and a nobler Thing than *Diligence.*

I would have them come to propound and expect, at this
rate, *I have done well, and now I will go to my Father; He
will teach me some curious Thing for it.* I must have them
count it a *Priviledge,* to be taught; and I sometimes manage
the Matter so, that my Refusing to teach them Something, is
their *Punishment.*

The *slavish* way of *Education,* carried on with raving and
kicking and scourging (in *Schools* as well as *Families,*) tis
abominable; and a dreadful Judgment of God upon the World.

VIII. Tho' I find it a marvellous Advantage to have the
Children strongly biased by Principles of *Reason* and *Honour,* (which, I find, Children will feel sooner than is com-

monly thought for:) yett I would neglect no Endeavours, to have *higher Principles* infused into them.

I therefore betimes awe them with the *Eye* of God upon them.

I show them, how they must love JESUS CHRIST; and show it, by doing what their Parents require of them.

I ofteñ tell them of the *good Angels,* who love them, and help them, and guard them; and who take Notice of them: and therefore must not be disobliged.

Heaven and *Hell,* I sett before them, as the Consequences of their Behaviour here.

IX. When the Children are capable of it, I take them *alone,* one by one; and after my Charges unto them, to fear God, and serve Christ, and shun Sin, *I pray with them* in my Study and make them the Witnesses of the Agonies, with which I address the Throne of Grace on their behalf.

X. I find much Benefit, by a particular Method, as of *Catechising* the Children, so of carrying the *Repetition* of the public Sermons unto them.

The Answers of the *Catechism* I still explain with abundance of brief *Quaestions,* which make them to take in the Meaning of it, and I see, that they do so.

And when the Sermons are to be *Repeated,* I chuse to putt every *Trust,* into a *Quaestion,* to be answered still, with *Yes,* or, *No.* In this way I awaken their *Attention,* as well as enlighten their *Understanding.* And in this way I have an Opportunity, to ask, *Do you desire such, or such a Grace of God?* and the like. Yea, I have an Opportunity to demand, and perhaps, to obtain their *Consent* unto the glorious Articles of the *New Covenant.* The Spirit of Grace may fall upon them in this Action; and they may be siez'd by Him, and Held as His *Temples,* thro' eternal Ages.

4. Susanna Wesley:
On the Education of Her Family (1732)

Susanna Wesley (1669-1742), mother of John Wesley, the founder of Methodism, was the daughter of a Presbyterian minister. She later chose to conform to the established Church, becoming an Anglican. Her husband, Samuel Wesley, was the Anglican rector at Epworth in Lincolnshire from 1695 to 1734, yet he, too, was descended from nonconformist parents and grandparents. Both his father and his grandfather were Puritans.

The Puritan heritage is deeply imprinted in the convictions of Susanna Wesley and is evident in the practices she employed in raising her own children. Her success can be measured by the personalities, beliefs, and achievements of her children.

EPWORTH, July 24, 1732

DEAR SON, — According to your desire, I have collected the principal rules I observed in educating my family.

The children were always put into a regular method of living, in such things as they were capable of, from their birth; as in dressing and undressing, changing their linen, etc. The first quarter commonly passes in sleep. After that they were, if possible, laid into their cradle awake, and rocked to sleep, and so they were kept rocking till it was time for them to awake. This was done to bring them to a regular course of sleeping, which at first was three hours in the morning and three in the afternoon: afterwards two hours, till they needed none at all. When turned a year old (and some before) they were taught to fear the rod and to cry softly, by which means they escaped abundance of correction which they might

---

Eliza Clarke, *Susanna Wesley* (Boston, Roberts Brothers, 1886), pp. 48–55.

otherwise have had; and that most odious noise of the crying of children was rarely heard in the house, but the family usually lived in as much quietness as if there had not been a child among them.

As soon as they were grown pretty strong they were confined to three meals a day. At dinner their little table and chairs were set by ours, where they could be overlooked; and they were suffered to eat and drink [small beer] as much as they would, but not to call for anything. If they wanted aught they used to whisper to the maid that attended them, who came and spake to me; and as soon as they could handle a knife and fork they were set to our table. They were never suffered to choose their meat, but always made to eat such things as were provided for the family. Mornings they always had spoon meat; sometimes at nights. But whatever they had, they were never permitted at those meals to eat of more than one thing, and of that sparingly enough. Drinking or eating between meals was never allowed, unless in case of sickness, which seldom happened. Nor were they suffered to go into the kitchen to ask anything of the servants when they were at meat: if it was known they did so, they were certainly beat, and the servants severely reprimanded. At six, as soon as family prayer was over, they had their supper; at seven the maid washed them, and beginning at the youngest, she undressed and got them all to bed by eight, at which time she left them in their several rooms awake, for there was no such thing allowed of in our house as sitting by a child till it fell asleep.

They were so constantly used to eat and drink what was given them, that when any of them was ill there was no difficulty in making them take the most unpleasant medicine; for they durst not refuse it, though some of them would presently throw it up. This I mention to show that a person may be taught to take anything, though it be never so much against his stomach.

In order to form the minds of children, the first thing to be done is to conquer their will and bring them to an obedient temper. To inform the understanding is a work of time, and must with children proceed by slow degrees, as they are able to bear it; but the subjecting the will is a thing that must be done at once, and the sooner the better; for by neglecting timely correction they will contract a stubbornness and obstinacy which are hardly ever after conquered, and never without using such severity as would be as painful to me as to the child. In the esteem of the world they pass for kind and indulgent whom I call cruel parents, who permit their children to get habits which they know must be afterwards broken. Nay, some are so stupidly fond as in sport to teach their children to do things which in a while after they have severely beaten them for doing. When a child is corrected it must be conquered, and this will be no hard matter to do, if it be not grown headstrong by too much indulgence. And when the will of a child is totally subdued, and it is brought to revere and stand in awe of the parents, then a great many childish follies and inadvertencies may be passed by. Some should be overlooked and taken no notice of, and others mildly reproved; but no wilful transgression ought ever to be forgiven children without chastisement less or more, as the nature of circumstances of the case may require. I insist on the conquering of the will of children betimes, because this is the only strong and rational foundation of a religious education, without which both precept and example will be ineffectual. But when this is thoroughly done, then a child is capable of being governed by the reason and piety of its parents till its own understanding comes to maturity, and the principles of religion have taken root in the mind.

I cannot yet dismiss the subject. As self-will is the root of all sin and misery, so whatever cherishes this in children insures their after wretchedness and irreligion: whatever checks and mortifies it, promotes their future happiness and piety. This is still more evident if we further consider that religion is nothing else than doing the will of God and not our own; that the one grand impediment to our temporal and eternal happiness being this self-will, no indulgence of it can be trivial, no denial unprofitable. Heaven or hell depends on this alone; so that the parent who studies to subdue it in his child works together with God in the renewing and saving a soul. The parent who indulges it does the Devil's work; makes religion impracticable, salvation unattainable, and does all that in him lies to damn his child body and soul forever.

Our children were taught as soon as they could speak, the Lord's prayer, which they were made to say at rising and at bedtime constantly; to which, as they grew bigger, were added a short prayer for their parents, and some collects, a short catechism, and some portion of Scripture, as their memories could bear. They were very early made to distinguish the Sabbath from other days, before they could well speak or go. They were as soon taught to be still at family prayers, and to ask a blessing immediately after, which they used to do by signs, before they could kneel or speak.

They were quickly made to understand they might have nothing they cried for, and instructed to speak handsomely for what they wanted. They were not suffered to ask even the lowest servant for aught without saying "Pray give me such a thing;" and the servant was chid if she ever let them omit that word.

Taking God's name in vain, cursing and swearing, profanity, obscenity, rude, ill-bred names, were never heard among them; nor were they ever permitted to call each other by their proper names without the addition of brother or sister.

There was no such thing as loud playing or talking allowed of, but every one was kept close to business for the six hours of school. And it is almost incredible what may be taught a child in a quarter of a year by a vigorous application, if it have but a tolerable capacity and good health. Kezzy excepted, all could read better in that time than the most of women can do as long as they live. Rising out of their places, or going out of the room, was not permitted except for good cause; and running into the yard, garden, or street, without leave, was always esteemed a capital offence.

For some years we went on very well. Never were children

in better order. Never were children better disposed to piety, or in more subjection to their parents, till that fatal dispersion of them after the fire into several families. In these they were left at full liberty to converse with servants, which before they had always been restrained from, and to run abroad to play with any children, bad or good. They soon learned to neglect a strict observance of the Sabbath, and got knowledge of several songs and bad things which before they had no notion of. That civil behavior which made them admired when they were at home by all who saw them was in a great measure lost, and a clownish accent and many rude ways were learned which were not reformed without some difficulty.

When the house was rebuilt, and the children all brought home, we entered on a strict reform; and then was begun the system of singing psalms at beginning and leaving school, morning and evening. Then also that of a general retirement at five o'clock was entered upon, when the eldest took the youngest that could speak, and the second the next, to whom they read the psalms for the day and a chapter of the New Testament, as in the morning they were directed to read the psalms and a chapter in the Old Testament, after which they went to their private prayers, before they got their breakfast or came into the family.

There were several by-laws observed among us. I mention them here because I think them useful.

First, it had been observed that cowardice and fear of punishment often lead children into lying till they get a custom of it which they cannot leave. To prevent this, a law was made that whoever was charged with a fault of which they were guilty, if they would ingenuously confess it and promise to amend should not be beaten. This rule prevented a great deal of lying, and would have done more if one in the family would have observed it. But he could not be prevailed upon, and therefore was often imposed on by false colors and equivocations which none would have used but one, had they been kindly dealt with; and some in spite of all would always speak truth plainly.

Second, that no sinful action, as lying, pilfering at church or on the Lord's Day, disobedience, quarrelling, etc., should ever pass unpunished.

Third, that no child should be ever chid or beat twice for the same fault, and that if they amended they should never be upbraided with it afterwards.

Fourth, that every signal act of obedience, especially when it crossed upon their own inclinations, should be always commended, and frequently rewarded according to the merits of the case.

Fifth, that if ever any child performed an act of obedience, or did anything with an intention to please, though the performance was not well, yet the obedience and intention should be kindly accepted, and the child with sweetness directed how to do better for the future.

Sixth, that propriety [the rights of property] be invariably preserved, and none suffered to invade the property of another in the smallest matter, though it were of the value of a farthing or a pin, which they might not take from the owner without, much less against, his consent. This rule can never be too much inculcated on the minds of children; and from the want of parents and governors doing it as they ought, proceeds that shameful neglect of justice which we may observe in the world.

Seventh, that promises be strictly observed; and a gift once bestowed, and so the right passed away from the donor, be not resumed, but left to the disposal of him to whom it was given, unless it were conditional, and the condition of the obligation not performed.

Eighth, that no girl be taught to work till she can read very well; and that she be kept to her work with the same application and for the same time that she was held to in reading. This rule also is much to be observed, for the putting children to learn sewing before they can read perfectly is the very reason why so few women can read fit to be heard, and never to be well understood.

SUSANNA WESLEY

5. John Wesley:
Sermon on the Education of Children
(Ca. 1783)

The historical importance of John Wesley (1703–1791), the principal founder of Methodism, has been enduring. Although both of his parents were members of the Church of England and he was raised as an Anglican, his family had been strongly Puritan throughout most of the 17th century. He himself never separated from the established church, but he was in many ways an 18th-century Puritan, echoing the nonconformity of his forefathers. He was educated at Charterhouse School and graduated from Christ Church College at Oxford in 1724; four years later he was ordained in the Church of England. Although he traveled as a missionary to Georgia and South Carolina between 1735 and 1738, his life was spent mostly in England, where he preached and traveled thousands of miles as an itinerant minister.

Deeply devoted to his mother, Wesley remained a bachelor until 1751, when he finally married a widow with four children. The marriage proved to be a disaster, and the couple separated without producing any children of their own. Whatever Wesley may have lacked in terms of practical experience as a father, he more than made up for by the intensity of his convictions about proper methods of child rearing. In doing so, he sustained the methods and the convictions that had been instrumental in shaping his own earliest years, as the letter written earlier by his mother, Susanna Wesley (reprinted in the preceding reading) makes amply clear.

SERMON C. ON THE EDUCATION OF CHILDREN

PROVERBS XXII. 6

*"Train up a Child in the Way wherein he should go, and
when he is old he will not depart from it."*

1. We must not imagine, that these words are to be understood in a absolute sense, as if no child that had been trained up in the way wherein he should go, had ever departed from it. Matter of fact will by no means agree with this. So far from it, that it has been a common observation, Some of the best parents have the worst children. It is true, this might sometimes be the case, because good men have not always a good understanding. And without this it is hardly to be expected, that they will know how to train up their children. Besides those who are, in other respects, good men, have often too much easiness of temper; so that they go no farther in restraining their children from evil, than old Eli did, when he said gently, "Nay, my sons, the report I hear of you is not good." This then is no contradiction to the assertion; for their children are not "trained up in the way wherein they should go." But it must be acknowledged, some have been trained therein with all possible care and diligence: and yet before they were old, yea, in the strength of their years, they did utterly depart from it.

2. The words then must be understood with some limitation, and then they contain an unquestionable truth. It is a general, though not a universal promise, and many have found the happy accomplishment of it. As this is the most probable method of making their children pious, which any parents can take, so it generally, although not always, meets with the desired success. The God of their fathers is with their children: he blesses their endeavours: and they have the

From *The Works of the Rev. John Wesley* (London: Thomas Cordeux, 1811), Vol. X, pp. 205-19.

satisfaction of leaving their religion, as well as their worldly substance, to those that descend from them.

3. But what is *the Way wherein* a child *should go?* And how shall we *train him up* therein? The ground of this is admirably well laid down by Mr. Law, in his *Serious Call to a devout Life*. Part of his words are. —

"Had we continued perfect, as God created the first man, perhaps the perfection of our nature had been a sufficient self-instructer for every one. But as sickness and diseases have created the necessity of medicines and physicians, so the disorders of our rational nature have introduced the necessity of education and tutors.

"And as the only end of a physician is, to restore nature to its own state, so the only end of education is, to restore our rational nature to its proper state. Education, therefore, is to be considered, as reason borrowed at secondhand, which is, as far as it can, to supply the loss of original perfection. And as physic may justly be called the art of restoring health, so education should be considered in no other light, than as the art of recovering to man his rational perfection.

"This was the end pursued by the youths that attended upon Pythagoras, Socrates, and Plato. Their every day lessons and instructions were so many lectures upon the nature of man, his true end, and the right use of his faculties: upon the immortality of the soul, its relation to God; the agreeableness of virtue to the divine nature; upon the necessity of temperance, justice, mercy, and truth, and the folly of indulging our passions.

"Now as Christianity has, as it were, new created the moral and religious world, and set every thing that is reasonable, wise, holy, and desirable, in its true point of light: so one would expect the education of children should be as much mended by Christianity, as the doctrines of religion are.

"As it has introduced a new state of things, and so fully informed us of the nature of man and the end of his creation: as it has fixed all our goods and evils, taught us the mean of purifying our souls, of pleasing God, and being happy eter-

either to the "desire of the flesh, the desire of the eyes, or the pride of life." "The desire of the flesh," is a propensity to seek happiness in what gratifies one or more of the outward senses. "The desire of the eyes" is a propensity to seek happiness in what gratifies the internal sense, the imagination, either by things grand, or new, or beautiful. "The pride of life" seems to mean a propensity to seek happiness in what gratifies the sense of honour. To this head is usually referred, *the love of money,* one of the basest passions that can have place in the human heart. But it may be doubted, whether this be not an acquired, rather than a natural distemper.

9. Whether this be a natural disease or not, it is certain, *anger* is. The ancient Philosopher defines it, "A sense of injury received, with a desire of revenge." Now, were there ever any one born of a woman, who did not labour under this? Indeed, like other diseases of the mind, it is far more violent in some than in others. But it is *furor brevis,* as the Poet speaks: it is a real, though short madness, wherever it is.

10. A deviation from *truth* is equally natural to all the children of men. One said in his haste, "All men are liars:" but we may say, upon cool reflection, All natural men will, upon a close temptation, vary from, or disguise the truth. If they do not offend against *veracity,* if they do not say what is false, yet they frequently offend against *simplicity.* They use art: they hang out false colours: they practise either simulation or dissimulation. So that you cannot say truly of any person living, till grace has altered nature, "Behold an Israelite indeed, in whom is no guile."

11. Every one is likewise prone by nature, to speak or act contrary to *justice.* This is another of the diseases which we bring with us into the world. All human creatures are naturally partial to themselves, and when opportunity offers, have more regard to their own interest or pleasure, than strict justice allows. Neither is any man by nature *merciful,* as our heavenly Father is merciful: but all, more or less, transgress that glorious rule of mercy as well as justice, "Whatsoever ye would that men should do unto you, the same do unto them."

12. Now if these are the general diseases of human nature, is it not the grand end of education to cure them? And is it not the part of all those to whom God has entrusted the education of children, to take all possible care, first, not to increase, not to feed any of these diseases, (as the generality of parents constantly do) and next to use every possible mean of healing them?

13. To come to particulars. What can parents do, and mothers more especially, to whose care our children are necessarily committed, in their tender years, with regard to the *Atheism* that is natural to all the children of men? How is this fed by the generality of parents, even those that love, or, at least, fear God, while in spending hours, perhaps days with their children, they hardly name the Name of God? Mean time, they talk of a thousand other things in the world that are round about them. Will not then the things of the present world, which surround these children on every side, naturally take up their thoughts, and set God at a greater distance from them, (if that be possible,) than he was before? Do not parents feed the Atheism of their children farther, by ascribing the works of creation to *nature?* Does not the common way of talking about nature leave God quite out of the question? Do they not feed this disease, whenever they talk in the hearing of their children, of any thing *happening* so or so? Of things coming by *chance?* Of good or ill *fortune?* As also when they ascribe this or that event, to the wisdom or power of men: or, indeed, to any other second causes, as if these governed the world? Yea, do they not feed it unawares, while they are talking of their own wisdom, or goodness, or power to do this or that, without expressly mentioning, that all these are the gifts of God? All tends to confirm the Atheism of their children and to keep God out of their thoughts.

14. But we are by no means clear of their blood, if we only go thus far, if we barely do not feed their disease. What can be done to cure it? From the first dawn of reason continually inculcate, God is in this and every place. God made you, and me, and the earth, and the sun, and the moon, and every

thing. And every thing is his: heaven, and earth, and all that is therein. God orders all things: He makes the sun shine, and the wind blow, and the trees bear fruit. Nothing comes by chance: that is a silly word: there is no such thing as chance. As God made the world, so he governs the world, and every thing that is in it, Not so much as a sparrow falls to the ground, without the Will of God. And as he governs all things, so he governs all men, good and bad, little and great. He gives them all the power and wisdom they have. And he over-rules all. He gives us all the goodness we have: every good thought, and word, and work, are from him. Without him we can neither think any thing right, or do any thing right. Thus it is, we are to inculcate upon them, That *God is all in all.*

15. Thus may we counteract, and, by the grace of God assisting us, gradually cure the natural Atheism of our children. But what can we do to cure their *Self-will?* It is equally rooted in their nature, and is, indeed, the original idolatry, which is not confined to one age or country, but is common to all the nations under heaven. And how few parents are to be found even among Christians, even among them that truly fear God, who are not guilty in this matter? Who do not continually feed and increase this grievous distemper in their children? To let them have their own will, does this most effectually. To let them take their own way, is the sure method of increasing their self-will sevenfold. But who has the resolution to do otherwise? One parent in one hundred? Who can be so singular, so cruel, as not, more or less, to *humour* her child? "And why should you not? What harm can there be in this, which every body does?" The harm is, that it strengthens their will more and more, till it will neither bow to God nor man. To humour children is, as far as in us lies, to make their disease incurable. A wise parent, on the other hand, should begin to break their will, the first moment it appears. In the whole art of Christian education there is nothing more important than this. The will of a parent is to a little child in the place of the will of God. Therefore, studi-

ously teach them to submit to this while they are children,
that they may be ready to submit to his will, when they are
men. But in order to carry this point, you will need incredible
firmness and resolution. For after you have once begun, you
must never more give way. You must hold on still in an even
course: you must never intermit your attention for one hour;
otherwise you will lose your labour.

16. If you are not willing to lose all the labour you have
been at, to break the will of your child, to bring his will into
subjection to yours, that it may be afterward subject to the
will of God, there is one advice, which, though little known,
should be particularly attended to. It may seem a small circumstance; but it is of more consequence than one can easily
imagine. It is this; never, on any account, give a child any
thing that it cries for. For it is a true observation, (and you
may make the experiment as often as you please,) If you give
a child what he cries for, you *pay him for crying:* and then he
will certainly cry again. "But if I do not give it him when he
cries, he will scream all day long." If he does, it is your own
fault; for it is in your power effectually to prevent it. For no
mother need suffer a child to cry aloud after it is a year old.
"Why, it is impossible to hinder it." So many suppose; but it
is an entire mistake. I am a witness of the direct contrary; and
so are many others. My own mother had ten children, each of
whom had spirit enough. Yet not one of them was ever heard
to cry aloud, after it was a year old. A gentlewoman of
Sheffield, (several of whose children I suppose are alive still,)
assured me, she had the same success with regard to her eight
children. When some were objecting to the possibility of this,
Mr. Parson Greenwood, (well known in the North of England,) replied, "This cannot be impossible; I have had the
proof of it in my own family. Nay, of more than this. I had six
children by my former wife. And she suffered none of them to
cry aloud, after they were ten months old. And yet none of
their spirits were so broken, as to unfit them for any of the
offices of life." This, therefore, may be done by any woman of
sense, who may thereby save herself abundance of trouble,

and prevent that disagreeable noise, the squawling of young children, from being heard under her roof. But I allow, none but a woman of sense will be able to effect this. Yea, and a woman of such patience and resolution, as only the grace of God can give. However, this is doubtless the more excellent way: and she that is able to receive it, let her receive it!

17. It is hard to say, whether self-will or *pride* be the more fatal distemper. It was chiefly pride that threw down so many of the stars of heaven, and turned angels into devils. But what can parents do, in order to check this until it can be radically cured?

First: Beware of adding fuel to the flame, of feeding the disease, which you should cure. Almost all parents are guilty of doing this, by praising their children to their face. If you are sensible of the folly and cruelty of this, see that you sacredly abstain from it. And in spite of either fear or complaisance, go one step farther. Not only do not encourage, but do not suffer others to do what you dare not do yourself. How few parents are sufficiently aware of this! Or, at least, sufficiently resolute to practise it. To check every one at the first word, that would praise them before their face. Even those who would not, on any account, *sit attentive to their own applause,* nevertheless, do not scruple to sit attentive to the applause of their children. Yea, and that to their face! O consider! Is not this the spreading a net for their feet? Is it not a grievous incentive to pride, even if they are praised for what is truly praise-worthy? Is it not doubly hurtful, if they are praised for things not truly praise-worthy;—things of an indifferent nature, as sense, good breeding, beauty, elegance of apparel? This is liable not only to hurt the heart, but their understanding also. It has a manifest and direct tendency, to infuse pride and folly together: to pervert both their taste and judgment, teaching them to value what is dung and dross in the sight of God.

18. If, on the contrary, you desire, without loss of time, to strike at the root of their pride, teach your children, as soon as possibly you can, that they are fallen spirits; that they are

fallen short of that glorious image of God, wherein they were
first created; that they are not now, as they were once, in-
corruptible pictures of the God of glory; bearing the express
likeness of the wise, the good, the holy Father of spirits; but
more ignorant, more foolish, and more wicked, than they can
possibly conceive. Shew them that, in pride, passion, and
revenge, they are now like the devil. And that in foolish
desires and grovelling appetites, they are like the beasts of the
field. Watch over them diligently in this respect, that whenever occasion offers, you may "pride in its earliest motions
find," and check the very first appearance of it.

If you ask, "But how shall I encourage them when they do
well, if I am never to commend them?" I answer, I did not
affirm this: I did not say, "You are *never* to commend them."
I know, many writers assert this, and writers of eminent
piety. They say, "To commend man, is to rob God," and
therefore condemn it altogether. But what say the Scriptures?
I read there, that our Lord himself frequently commended his
own disciples: and the great Apostle scruples not to commend the Corinthians, Philippians, and divers others to whom
he writes. We may not, therefore, condemn this altogether.
But I say, use it exceeding sparingly. And when you use it,
let it be with the utmost caution, directing them at the same
moment, to look upon all they have as a free gift of God, and
with the deepest self-abasement to say, "Not unto us! Not
unto us! but unto thy Name give the praise!"

19. Next to self-will and pride, the most fatal disease with
which we are born, is *love of the world*. But how studiously
do the generality of parents cherish this in its several
branches? They cherish "the desire of the flesh," that is, the
tendency to seek happiness in pleasing the outward senses,
by studying to *enlarge the pleasure of tasting* in their children
to the uttermost: not only giving them before they are weaned
other things beside milk, the natural food of children, but
giving them both before and after, any sort of meat or drink
that they will take. Yea, they entice them long before nature
requires it, to take wine or strong drink: and provide them

with comfits, gingerbread, raisins, and whatever fruit they have a mind to. They feed in them "the desire of the eyes," the propensity to seek happiness in pleasing the imagination, by giving them pretty playthings, glittering toys, shining buckles, or buttons, fine clothes, red shoes, laced hats, needless ornaments, as ribbons, necklaces, ruffles: yea, and by proposing any of these as *rewards* for doing their duty, which is stamping a great value upon them. With equal care and attention they cherish in them the third branch of the love of the world, *the pride of life,* the propensity to seek their happiness in the "honour that cometh of men." Nor is the love of money forgotten: many an exhortation do they hear, on *securing the main chance;* many a lecture exactly agreeing with that of the old Heathen, *"Si possis, recte; si non, quocunque modo rem."* "Get money, honestly if you can; but if not; get money." And they are carefully taught to look on riches and honour as the reward of all their labours.

20. In direct opposition to all this, a wise and truly kind parent will take the utmost care, not to cherish in her children the desire of the flesh, their natural propensity to seek happiness in gratifying the outward senses. With this view she will suffer them to taste no food but milk, till they are weaned; which a thousand experiments shew is most safely and easily done at the seventh month. And then accustom them to the most simple food, chiefly of vegetables. She may inure them to taste only one kind of food, beside bread, at dinner, and constantly to breakfast and sup on milk, either cold, or heated; but not boiled. She may use them to sit by her at meals; and ask for nothing, but take what is given them. She need never, till they are, at least, nine or ten years old, let them know the taste of tea, or use any other drink at meals, but water, or small beer. And they will never desire to taste either meat or drink between meals, if not accustomed thereto. If fruit, comfits, or any thing of the kind be given them, let them not touch it but at meals. And never propose any of these as a reward; but teach them to look higher than this.

But herein a difficulty will arise, which it will need much

resolution to conquer. Your servants who will not understand
your plan, will be continually giving little things to your
children, and thereby undoing all your work. This you must
prevent, if possible, by warning them when they first come
into your house, and repeating the warning from time to time.
If they *will* do it notwithstanding, you must turn them away.
Better lose a good servant than spoil a good child.

Possibly you may have another difficulty to encounter, and
one of a still more trying nature. Your mother, or your husband's mother, may live with you; and you will do well to
shew her all possible respect. But let her on no account have
the least share in the management of your children. She
would undo all that you have done; she would give them their
own will in all things. She would humour them to the destruc-
tion of their souls, if not their bodies too. In four-score years
I have not met with one woman that knew how to manage
grand-children. My own mother, who governed her children
so well, could never govern one grand-child. In every other
point obey your mother. Give up your will to her's. But with
regard to the management of your children, steadily keep the
reins in your own hands.

21. A wise and kind parent will be equally cautious, of
feeding "the desire of the eyes" in her children. She will give
them no pretty play things, no glittering toys, shining buckles
or buttons, fine or gay clothes: no needless ornaments of any
kind; nothing that can attract the eye. Nor will she suffer any
other person to give them what she will not give them herself.
Any thing of the kind that is offered, may be either civilly
refused, or received and laid by. If they are displeased at this,
you cannot help it. Complaisance, yea, and temporal interest,
must needs be set aside, when the eternal interests of your
children are at stake.

Your pains will be well requited, if you can inspire them
early, with a contempt of all finery; and on the other hand,
with a love and esteem, for neat plainness of dress. Teaching
them to associate the ideas of plainness and modesty: and
those of a fine and a loose woman. Likewise, instill into them

as early as possible, a fear and contempt of pomp and grandeur, and abhorrence and dread of the love of money, and a deep conviction, that riches cannot give happiness. Wean them, therefore, from all these false ends: habituate them to make God their end in all things, and inure them in all they do, to aim at knowing, loving, and serving God.

22. Again: The generality of parents feed *anger* in their children, yea, the worst part of it, that is, revenge. The silly mother says, "What hurt my child! Give me a blow for it." What horrid work is this! Will not the old murderer teach them this lesson fast enough? Let the Christian parent spare no pains to teach them just the contrary. Remind them of the words of our blessed Lord, "It was said of old, An eye for an eye, and a tooth for a tooth. But I say unto you, that ye resist not evil." Not by returning evil for evil. Rather than this, "if a man take away thy cloak, let him take away thy coat also." Remind him of the words of the great Apostle, "Dearly beloved, Avenge not yourselves. For it is written, Vengeance is mine: I will repay, saith the Lord."

23. The generality of parents feed and increase the natural *falsehood* of their children. How often may we hear that senseless word! "No, it was not *you;* it was not my child that did it: say, it was the cat." What amazing folly is this! Do you feel no remorse, while you are putting a lie in the mouth of your child, before it can speak plainly? And do not you think, it will make a good proficiency when it comes to years of discretion? Others teach them both dissimulation and lying, by their unreasonable severity: and yet others, by admiring and applauding their ingenious lies and cunning tricks. Let the wise parent on the contrary, teach them to "put away all lying," and both in little things and great, in jest or earnest, speak the very truth from their heart. Teach them that the author of all falsehood is the devil, who "is a liar and the father of it." Teach them to abhor and despise, not only lying, but all equivocating, all cunning and dissimulation. Use every mean to give them a love of truth: of veracity, sincerity, and simplicity, and of openness both of spirit and behaviour.

24. Most parents increase the natural tendency to *injustice* in their children, by conniving at their wronging each other, if not laughing at, or even applauding their witty contrivances to cheat one another. Beware of every thing of this kind: and from their very infancy, sow the seeds of justice in their hearts; and train them up in the exactest practice of it. If possible, teach them the love of justice, and that in the least things as well as the greatest. Impress upon their minds the old proverb, "He that will steal a penny, will steal a pound." Habituate them to render unto all their due, even to the uttermost farthing.

25. Many parents connive, likewise, at the *ill-nature* of their children, and thereby strengthen it. But truly affectionate parents will not indulge them in any kind or degree of *unmercifulness*. They will not suffer them to vex their brothers or sisters, either by word or deed. They will not allow them to hurt or give pain to any thing that has life. They will not permit them to rob birds-nests, must less to kill any thing without necessity: not even snakes, which are as innocent as worms, or toads, which, notwithstanding their ugliness, and the ill name they lie under, have been proved over and over, to be as harmless as flies. Let them extend in its measure, the rule of doing as they would be done by, to every animal whatsoever. Ye that are truly kind parents; in the morning, in the evening, and all the day beside, press upon all your children, "to walk in love, as Christ also loved us, and gave himself for us;" to mind that one point, "God is love: and he that dwelleth in love, dwelleth in God, and God in Him."

6.   Jonathan Edwards:
Observations of His Family (1765, 1829)

By a remarkable coincidence, the two men who dominated evangelicalism in England and America in the 18th centu- ry — John Wesley and Jonathan Edwards — were born in the same year, 1703. Like Wesley in England, Jonathan Edwards (1703-1758) epitomizes the central beliefs and emotional ex- periences of 18th-century American evangelicalism. In his ser- mons and writings (including three brilliant treatises on *Origi- nal Sin, Religious Affections,* and *Freedom of the Will*), Ed- wards was an acute analyst of religious experiences, partic- ularly those that reflected a Calvinist nature.

Edwards believed, as did other Puritan-Evangelicals, that Christians ought to be humble, self-denying, mortified men and women, whose personal wills were entirely devoted to the fulfillment of the will of God. Conversion, or religious rebirth, was central to their commitment to a pure church, comprised solely of people who had received saving grace from God and thus established their positions as Christian saints, elected to salvation.

Although Jonathan Edwards never wrote a specific treatise on education and child rearing, his own methods of raising his children and disciplining his family were observed and com- mented upon by several writers. It is thus possible to discover the practices of one of the most eminent American ministers of the 18th century and to see how he sought to shape the personalities of his own children according to the dictates of his religious beliefs and goals.

68	CHILD-REARING CONCEPTS: HISTORICAL SOURCES

A. AS SEEN BY SAMUEL HOPKINS

His General Manner of Life

MR. EDWARDS made a secret of his private devotion, and
therefore it cannot be particularly known; though there is
much evidence that he was punctual, constant, and frequent
in secret prayer, and often kept days of fasting and prayer in
secret and set apart time for serious devout meditations on
spiritual and eternal things, as part of his religious exercise in
secret. It appears by his Diary, that in his youth he determined to attend secret prayer more than twice a-day, when
circumstances would allow. He was, so far as can be known,
much on his knees in secret, and in devout reading God's
word and meditation upon it. And his constant solemn converse with God in these exercises of secret religion made his
face, as it were, to shine before others. His appearance, his
countenance, words, and whole demeanour, (though without
any thing of affected grimace and sour austerity,) was attended with a seriousness, gravity, and solemnity, which was
the natural, genuine indication, and expression of a deep,
abiding sense of divine things on his mind, and of his living
constantly in the fear of God.

Agreeable to his Resolutions, he was very careful and
abstemious in eating and drinking, as doubtless it was necessary so great a student, and a person of so delicate and tender
a bodily make as he was, should be, in order to be comfortable and useful. When he had, by careful observation, found
what kind and what quantity of diet best suited his constitution, and rendered him most fit to pursue his work, he
was very strict and exact in complying with it; and in this
respect *lived by rule;* and herein constantly practiced great
self-denial, which he also did in his constant early rising, in

From Samuel Hopkins, *The Life and Character of the Late Reverend,
Learned, and Pious Mr. Jonathan Edwards, President of the College of
New-Jersey. Together with Extracts from his Private Writings & Diary. And
Also Seventeen Select Sermons on Various Important Subjects* (North-
ampton, Mass., Andrew Wright for S. and E. Butler, 1804), pp. 42–49, 57.

order to redeem time for his study. He used himself to rise by four, or between four and five in the morning.

Though he was of a tender and delicate constitution, yet few students are capable of close application more hours in a day than he: He commonly spent thirteen hours every day in his study. His most usual diversion, in summer, was riding on horseback and walking. He would commonly, unless diverted by company, ride two or three miles after dinner to some lonely grove, where he would dismount and walk a while. At which times he generally carried his pen and ink with him, to note any thought that should be suggested, which he chose to retain and pursue, as what promised some light on any important subject. In the winter he was wont almost daily to take an axe and chop wood moderately, for the space of half an hour or more.

He had an uncommon thirst for knowledge; in the pursuit of which he spared no cost nor pains. He read all the books, especially books of divinity, that he could come at, from which he could hope to get any help in his pursuit of knowledge. And in this, he confined not himself to authors of any particular sect or denomination; yea, took much pains to come at the books of the most noted writers, who advance a scheme of divinity most contrary to his own principles. But he studied the Bible more than all other books, and more than most other divines do. His uncommon acquaintance with the Bible appears in his sermons, and in most of his publications: and his great pains in studying it are manifest in his manuscript notes upon it; of which a more particular account may be given hereafter. He took his religious principles from the Bible, and not from any human system or body of divinity. Though his principles were *Calvinistic,* yet he called no man father. He thought and judged for himself, and was truly very much of an original. This is evident by what he published in his life-time, and is yet more so by his MSS. . . . For reading was not the only method he took to improve his mind; but he did this much by writing; without which it is probable, no student can make improvements to the best advantage.

Agreeable to Resolution 11, he applied himself with all his mind to find out the truth: he searched for understanding and knowledge, as for silver, and digged for it, as for hid treasures. Every thought, on any subject which appeared to him worth pursuing and preserving, he pursued, as far as he then could, with his pen in his hand. Thus he was all his days, like the busy bee, collecting from every opening flower, and storing up a flock of knowledge, which was indeed sweet to him, as the honey and the honey-comb. And as he advanced in years and in knowledge, his pen was more and more employed, and his manuscripts grew much faster on his hands.

He was thought by some, who had but a slight acquaintance with him, to be stiff and unsociable: but this was owing to want of better acquaintance. He was not a man of many words indeed, and was somewhat reserved among strangers, and those on whose candour and friendship he did not know he could rely. And this was probably owing to two things: *First,* the strict guard he set over his tongue from his youth, which appears by his Resolutions, taking great care never to use it in any way that might prove mischievous to any: never to *sin with his tongue;* nor to improve it in idle, trivial, and impertinent talk, which generally makes up a great part of the conversation of those who are full of words in all companies. He was sensible, that in the multitude of words there wanteth not sin; and therefore refrained his lips, and habituated himself to *think* before he spoke, and to propose some good end even in all his words; which led him to be above many others, agreeable to St James's advice, *slow to speak. Secondly,* This was in part the effect of his bodily constitution. He possessed but a comparative small stock of animal life: his animal spirits were low, and he had not strength of lungs to spare, that would be necessary in order to make him what would be called, an affable, facetious gentleman, in all companies. They who have a great flow of animal spirits, and so can speak with more ease and less expence, may doubtless lawfully practice free conversation in all companies for a lower end, (*e.g.* to please and render themselves acceptable,) than he, who has not such a stock to expend upon. It becomes *him* to reserve what he has for higher and more important service. Besides, the want of animal spirits lays a man under a *natural* inability to that freedom of conversation at all times, and in whatever company he is, which those of more life naturally go into; and the greatest degree of sociable disposition, humility, and benevolence, will not remove this obstacle.

He was not forward to enter into any dispute among strangers, and in companies where were persons of different sentiments; as he was sensible that such disputes are generally unprofitable, and often sinful, and of bad consequence; and he thought he could dispute to the best advantage with his pen in his hand: yet he was always free to give his sentiments on any subject proposed to him, and remove any difficulties or objections offered by way of inquiry, as lying in the way of what he looked upon to be the truth. But how groundless the imputation of *stiff* and *unsociable* was, his known and tried friends best knew. They always found him easy of access, kind and condescending; and though not talkative, yet affable and free. Among such whose candour and friendship he had experienced he threw off the reserve, and was most open and free; quite patient of contradiction, while the utmost opposition was made to his sentiments, that could be by any plausible arguments or objections. And, indeed, he was, on all occassions, quite sociable and free with all who had any special business with him.

In his conduct in his family, he practised that conscientious exactness which was perspicuous in all his ways. He maintained a great esteem and regard for his amiable and excellent consort. Much of the tender and kind was expressed in his conversation with her, and conduct towards her. He was wont frequently to admit her into his study, and converse freely with her on matters of religion; and he used commonly to pray with her in his study, as least once a-day, unless something extraordinary prevented. The time in which this used to be commonly attended, was just before going to bed, after prayers in the family. As he rose very early himself, he

was wont to have his family up in season in the morning; after
which, before the family entered on the business of the day,
he attended on family prayers; when a chapter in the Bible
was read, commonly by candle-light in the winter; upon
which he asked his children questions according to their age
and capacity; and took occasion to explain some passages in
it, or enforce any duty recommended, &c. as he thought most
proper.

He was careful and thorough in the government of his
children; and, as a consequence of this, they reverenced,
esteemed, and loved him. He took special care to begin his
government of them in season. When they first discovered
any considerable degree of will and stubbornness, he would
attend to them till he had thoroughly subdued them and
brought them to submit. And such prudent thorough discipline, exercised with the greatest calmness, and commonly
without striking a blow, being repeated once or twice, was
generally sufficient for that child; and effectually established
his parental authority, and produced a cheerful obedience
ever after.

He kept a watchful eye over his children, that he might
admonish them of the *first* wrong step, and direct them in the
right way. He took opportunities to treat with them in his
study, singly and particularly, about their own soul's concerns; and to give them warning, exhortation, and direction,
as he saw occasion. He took much pains to instruct them in
the principles of religion; in which he made use of the *Assem-
bly's Shorter Catechism:* not merely by taking care that they
learned it by heart, but by leading them into an understanding
of the doctrines therein taught, by asking them questions on
each answer, and explaining it to them. His usual time to
attend this was on the evening before the Sabbath. And, as he
believed that the Sabbath, or holy time, began at sun-set the
evening before the day, he ordered his family to finish all their
secular business by that time, or before; when they were all
called together, and a psalm was sung and prayer attended, as
an introduction to the sanctifying the Sabbath. This care and

exactness effectually prevented that intruding on holy time, by attending on secular business, too common in families where the evening beforethe Sabbath is pretended to be observed.

He was a great enemy to young people's unseasonable company-keeping and frolicking, as he looked upon it as a great means of corrupting and ruining youth. And he thought the excuse many parents make for tolerating their children in it, (viz. that it is the custom, and others children practice it, which renders it difficult, and even impossible to restrain theirs,) was insufficient and frivolous; and manifested a great degree of stupidity, on supposition the practice was hurtful and pernicious to their souls. And when some of his children grew up he found no difficulty in restraining them from this pernicious practice; but they cheerfully complied with the will of their parents herein. He allowed not his children to be from home after nine o'clock at night, when they went abroad to see their friends and companions; neither were they allowed to sit up much after that time, in his own house, when any came to make them a visit. If any gentleman desired acquaintance with his daughters, after handsomely introducing himself, by properly consulting the parents, he was allowed all proper opportunity for it, and a room and fire, if needed: but must not intrude on the proper hours of rest and sleep, nor the religion and order of the family.

He had a strict and inviolable regard to justice in all his dealings with his neighbours, and was very careful to provide for things honest in the sight of all men; so that scarcely a man had any dealings with him, that was not conscious of his uprightness. He appeared to have a sacred regard to truth in his words, both in promises and narrations, agreeable to his Resolutions. This doubtless was one reason why he was not so full of words as many are: No man feared to rely on his veracity.

He was cautious in chusing his intimate friends, and therefore had not many that might properly be called such; but to them he shewed himself friendly in a peculiar manner. He was indeed a faithful friend, and able above most others to keep a secret. To them he discovered himself more than to others; led them into his views and ends in his conduct in particular instances; by which they had abundant evidence that he well understood human nature, and that his general reservedness, and many particular instances of his conduct, which a stranger might impute to ignorance of men, were really owing to his uncommon knowledge of mankind.

• • • • •

Mr. Edwards was what by some is called a rigid Calvinist. Those doctrines of Calvinism, which have been most objected against, and given the greatest offence, appeared to him as scriptural, reasonable, and important as any; and he thought, that to give them up was in effect to give up all. And therefore he looked upon those who called themselves Calvinists, that were for palliating the matter, by, as it were, trimming off the knots of Calvinism, that they might conform it more to the taste of those who are most disposed to object against it, were really giving up and betraying the cause they pretended to espouse; and were paving the way, not only to Arminianism, but to Deism. For if these doctrines, in the whole length and breadth of them, were relinquished, he did not see where a man could set his foot down, with consistency and safety, short of Deism, or even Atheism itself, or rather universal Scepticism.

B. AS SEEN BY SERENO E. DWIGHT

It was a peculiarly favourable dispensation of Providence, that, amid the multiplied cares and labours of this period, the health of Mr. Edwards was graciously preserved. A revival of religion to a clergyman, like the period of harvest to the husbandman, is the most busy and the most exhausting of all seasons; and during the progress of that, which he had just

From Sereno E. Dwight, (ed.), *The Works of President Edwards: With a Memoir of His Life* (New York: S. Converse, 1829), Vol. I, pp. 126–30.

witnessed, not only was the whole time of Mr. Edwards fully occupied, but all the powers of his mind were laboriously employed, and all the feelings of his heart kept, from month to month, in high and powerful excitement. In addition to his ordinary duties as a teacher and pastor, his public lectures were now multiplied, private lectures were weekly appointed in different parts of the town, and his study was almost daily thronged by multitudes, looking to him as their spiritual guide. From the adjacent villages, also, great numbers resorted to him, for the same purpose, having the highest confidence in his wisdom and experience; and numerous clergymen from various parts of the country, came to his house, to witness the triumphs of divine grace, and to gain, from his counsels and his measures, more just conceptions of the best manner of discharging the highest and most sacred duties of their office.

In the midst of these complicated labours, as well as at all times, he found at home one, who was in every sense a *help meet* for him; one who made their common dwelling the abode of order and neatness, of peace and comfort, of harmony and love, to all its inmates, and of kindness and hospitality to the friend, the visitant and the stranger. "While she uniformly paid a becoming deference to her husband, and treated him with entire respect, she spared no pains in conforming to his inclinations, and rendering every thing in the family agreeable and pleasant: accounting it her greatest glory, and that wherein she could best serve God and her generation, to be the means, in this way, of promoting his usefulness and happiness. As he was of a weakly, infirm constitution, and was necessarily peculiarly exact in his diet, she was a tender nurse to him, cheerfully attending upon him at all times, and in all things ministering to his comfort. And no person of discernment could be conversant in the family, without observing, and admiring, the perfect harmony, and mutual love and esteem, that subsisted between them. At the same time, when she herself laboured under bodily disorders and pains, which was not unfrequently the case, instead of troubling those around her with her complaints, and wearing a sour or dejected countenance, as if out of humour with every body, and every thing around her, because she was disregarded and neglected; she was accustomed to bear up under them, not only with patience, but with cheerfulness and good humour."

Devoted as Mr. Edwards was to study, and to the duties of his profession, it was necessary for him at all times, but especially in a season like this, of multiplied toils and anxieties, to be relieved from attention to all secular concerns; and it was a most happy circumstance, that he could trust every thing of this nature to the care of Mrs. Edwards, with entire safety, and with undoubting confidence. "She was a most judicious and faithful mistress of a family, habitually industrious, a sound economist, managing her household affairs with diligence and discretion. She was conscientiously careful, that nothing should be wasted and lost; and often, when she herself took care to save any thing *of trifling value,* or directed her children or others to do so, or when she saw them *waste* any thing, she would repeat the words of our Saviour—"THAT NOTHING BE LOST;" which words, she said she often thought of, as containing a maxim worth remembering, especially when considered as the reason alleged by Christ, why his disciples should gather up the fragments of that bread, which he had just before *created with a word.* She took almost the whole direction of the temporal affairs of the family, without doors and within, managing them with great wisdom and prudence, as well as cheerfulness; and in this, was particularly suited to the disposition, as well as the habits and necessities, of her husband, who chose to have no care, if possible, of any worldly business.

But there are other duties, of a still more tender and difficult nature, which none but a parent can adequately perform; and it was an unspeakable privilege to Mr. Edwards, now surrounded by a young and growing family, that when his duties to his people, especially in seasons like this, necessarily occupied his whole attention, he could safely commit

his children to the wisdom and piety, the love and faithfulness, of their mother. Her views of the responsibility of
parents, were large and comprehensive. "She thought that, as
a parent, she had great and important duties to do towards
her children, before they were capable of government and
instruction. For them, she constantly and earnestly prayed,
and bore them on her heart before God, in all her secret and
most solemn addresses to him: and that, even before they
were born. The prospect of her becoming the mother of a
rational immortal creature, which came into existence in an
undone and infinitely dreadful state, was sufficient to lead her
to bow before God daily, for his blessing on it — even redemption and eternal life by Jesus Christ. So that, through all the
pain, labour and sorrow, which attended her being the mother
of children, she was in travail for them, that they might be
born of God."

She regularly prayed with her children, from a very early
period, and, as there is the best reason to believe, with great
earnestness and importunity. Being thoroughly sensible that,
in many respects, the chief care of forming children by government and instruction, naturally lies on mothers, as they are
most with their children, at an age when they commonly
receive impressions that are permanent, and have great
influence in forming the character for life, she was very careful to do her part in this important business. When she fore-
saw, or met with, any special difficulty in this matter, she was
wont to apply to her husband, for advice and assistance; and
on such occasions, they would both attend to it, as a matter of
the utmost importance. She had an excellent way of governing her children; she knew how to make them regard and
obey her cheerfully, without loud angry words, much less
heavy blows. She seldom punished them; and in speaking to
them, used gentle and pleasant words. If any correction was
necessary, she did not administer it in a passion; and when
she had occasion to reprove and rebuke, she would do it in
few words, without warmth and noise, and with all calmness
and gentleness of mind. In her directions and reproofs in

matters of importance, she would address herself to the reason of her children, that they might not only know her inclination and will, but at the same time be convinced of the
reasonableness of it. She had need to speak but once; she was
cheerfully obeyed: murmuring and answering again, were not
known among them. In their manners, they were uncom-
monly respected to their parents. When their parents came
into the room, they all rose instinctively from their seats, and
never resumed them until their parents were seated; and
when either parent was speaking, no matter with whom they
had been conversing, they were all immediately silent and
attentive. The kind and gentle treatment they received from
their mother, while she strictly and punctiliously maintained
her parental authority, seemed naturally to beget and promote
a filial respect and affection, and to lead them to a mild tender
treatment of each other. Quarrelling and contention, which
too frequently take place among children, were in her family
wholly unknown. She carefully observed the first appearance
of resentment and ill will in her young children, towards any
person whatever, and did not connive at it, as many who have
the care of children do, but was careful to show her displeasure, and suppress it to the utmost; yet, not by angry,
wrathful words, which often provoke children to wrath, and
stir up their irascible passions, rather than abate them. Her
system of discipline, was begun at a very early age, and it was
her rule, to resist the first, as well as every subsequent exhibition of temper or disobedience in the child, however young,
until its will was brought into submission to the will of its
parents: wisely reflecting, that until a child will obey his
parents, he can never be brought to obey God.

Fond as Mr. Edwards was of welcoming the friend and the
stranger, and much as his house was a favourite place of
resort, to gentlemen both of the clergy and laity; it was
absolutely necessary, at all times, and peculiarily so in seasons of religious attention like this, that some one, well knowing how to perform the rites of hospitality, and to pay all the
civilities and charities of life, should relieve him from these

attentions, during those hours which were consecrated to his professional duties; and here also he could most advantageously avail himself of the assistance of Mrs. Edwards. Educated in the midst of polished life, familiar from childhood with the rules of decorum and good breeding, affable and easy in her manners, and governed by the feelings of liberality and benevolence, she was remarkable for her kindness to her friends, and to the visitants who resorted to Mr. Edwards; sparing no pains to make them welcome, and to provide for their convenience and comfort. She was also peculiarly kind to strangers, who came to her house. By her sweet and winning manners, and ready conversation, she soon became acquainted with them, and brought them to feel acquainted with herself; and showed such concern for their comfort, and so kindly offered what she thought they needed, that while her friendly attentions discovered at once that she knew the feelings of a stranger, they also made their way directly to his heart, and gained his confidence, led him immediately to feel as if he were at home, in the midst of near and affectionate friends.

"She made it her rule, to speak well of all, so far as she could with truth, and justice to herself and others. She was not wont to dwell with delight on the imperfections and failings of any; and when she heard persons speaking ill of others, she would say what she thought she could, with truth and justice, in their excuse, or divert the obloquy, by mentioning those things, that were commendable in them. Thus she was tender of every one's character, even of those who injured and spoke evil of her; and carefully guarded against the too common vice, of evil speaking and backbiting. She could bear injuries and reproach, with great calmness, without any disposition to render evil for evil; but, on the contrary, was ready to pity and forgive those, who appeared to be her enemies." This course of conduct, steadily pursued, secured, in an unusual degree, the affection and confidence of those who knew her.

She proved also, an invaluable auxiliary to Mr. Edwards, in

the duties of his profession, not only in her excellent example, but by her active efforts in doing good. "She was," says Dr. Hopkins, "eminent for her piety, and for experimental religion. Religious conversation was her delight; and, as far as propriety permitted, she promoted it in all companies. Her religious conversation showed at once, her clear comprehension of spiritual and divine things, and the deep impression which they had made upon her mind." It was not merely conversation *about* religion—about its truths, or duties, or its actual state—its doctrines or triumphs—or the character and conduct of its friends and ministers: it was religion itself;—that supreme love to God, to his kingdom and his glory, which, abounding in the heart, flows forth spontaneously, in the daily conversation and the daily life.

7. John Witherspoon:
Letters on Education (1797)

John Witherspoon (1723–1794) was born in Scotland and raised as a rigorous Calvinist Presbyterian. He became an important theologian, committed to the preservation of the old ways and beliefs of his church. In 1768, he accepted the invitation to come to America to serve as President of Princeton College, a position he retained until his death.

Although he was sympathetic to the views of the evangelicals of the New Light persuasion, he opposed the rigorous doctrines of the New Divinity men. In his political roles, he was firmly committed to the revolutionary Whigs, serving as a member of the New Jersey Constitutional Convention in 1776 and for several years as a representative to the Continental Congress. In his life and thought, he linked together Scottish and American religious doctrines with the prescriptions for education and the raising of children which are evident in the following selection.

LETTER I

AFTER so long a delay, I now set myself to fulfil my promise of writing to you a few thoughts on the education of children. Though I cannot wholly purge myself of the crimes of laziness and procrastination, yet I do assure you, what contributed not a little to its being hitherto not done, was, that I considered it not as an ordinary letter, but what deserved to be carefully meditated on, and thoroughly digested. The concern you show on this subject is highly commendable; for there is no part of your duty, as a Christian or a citizen, which will be of greater service to the Public, or a source of greater comfort to yourself.

The consequence of my thinking so long upon it, before committing my thoughts to paper, will probably be the taking the thing in a greater compass than either of us at first intended, and writing a series of letters instead of one. With this view I begin with a preliminary to the successful education of children, viz. that husband and wife ought to be entirely one upon this subject, not only agreed as to the end, but as to the means to be used, and the plan to be followed in order to attain it. . . . When this is the case, every thing is enforced by a double authority, and recommended by a double example; but when it is otherwise, the pains taken are commonly more than lost, not being able to do any good, and certainly producing very much evil.

Be pleased to remember, that this is by no means intended against those unhappy couples, who, being essentially different in principles and character, live in a state of continual war. It is of little advantage to speak either to, or of such persons. But even differences incomparably smaller are of very bad consequence: when one, for example, thinks a child

From *The Works of John Witherspoon, D.D. Sometime Minister of the Gospel at Paisley, and Late President of Princeton College, in New Jersey. Containing Essays, Sermons, &c. on Important Subjects; Intended to Illustrate and Establish the Doctrine of Salvation by Grace, and to Point Out Its Influence on Holiness of Life* (Edinburgh, Scotland: J. Ritchie, 1805), Vol. VIII, pp. 165–89.

may be carried out, and the other thinks it is wrong: when
one thinks a way of speaking is dangerous, and the other is
positive there is nothing in it. The things themselves may
indeed be of little moment, but the want of concurrence in the
parents, or the want of mutual esteem and deference, easily
observed even by very young children, is of the greatest
importance.

As you and I have chiefly in view the religious education of
children, I take it to be an excellent preliminary, that parental
affection should be purified by the principles, and controuled
or directed by the precepts of religion. A parent should rejoice in his children, as they are the gift of a gracious God;
should put his trust in the care of an indulgent Providence, for
the preservation of his offspring as well as himself; should be
supremely desirous that they may be, in due time, the heirs of
eternal life; and, as he knows the absolute dependence of
every creature upon the will of God, should be ready to
resign them at what time his Creator shall see proper to
demand them. This happy qualification of parental tenderness, will have a powerful influence in preventing mistakes in
the conduct of education. It will be the most powerful of all
incitements to duty, and at the same time a restraint upon that
natural fondness and indulgence which, by a sort of fascina-
tion or fatality, makes parents often do or permit what their
judgment condemns, and then excuse themselves by saying,
that no doubt it is wrong, but truly they cannot help it.

Another preliminary to the proper education of children is,
a firm persuasion of the benefit of it, and the probable, at
least, if not certain success of it, when faithfully and
prudently conducted. This puts an edge upon the spirit, and
enables the Christian not only to make some attempts, but to
persevere with patience and diligence. I know not a common
saying either more false or pernicious than "that the children
of good men are as bad as others." This saying carries in it a
supposition that whereas the force of education is confessed
with respect to every other human character and accomplishment, it is of no consequence at all as to religion. This, I

think, is contrary to daily experience. Where do we expect to find young persons piously disposed but in pious families? The exceptions, or rather appearances to the contrary, are easily accounted for in more ways than one. Many persons appear to be religious, while they are not so in reality, but are chiefly governed by the applause of men. Hence their visible conduct may be specious, or their public performances applauded, and yet their families be neglected.

It must also be acknowledged, that some truly well-disposed persons are extremely defective or imprudent in this part of their duty, and therefore it is no wonder that it should not succeed. This was plainly the case with Eli, whose sons, we are told, made themselves vile, and he restrained them not. However, I must observe, if we allow such to be truly good men, we must at the same time confess, that this was a great drawback upon their character; and that they differed very much from the father of the faithful, who had this honourable testimony given him by God, "I know him, that he will command his children, and his household after him, that they serve me." To this we may add, that the child of a good man, who is seen to follow dissolute courses, draws the attention of mankind more upon him, and is much more talked of, than any other person of the same character. Upon the whole, it is certainly of moment, that one who desires to educate his children in the fear of God, should do it in a humble persuasion, that if he is not defective in his own duty, he will not be denied the blessing of success. I could tell you some remarkable instances of parents who seemed to labour in vain for a long time, and yet were happy as to see a change at last; and of some children in whom, even after the death of the parents, the seed which was early sown, and seemed to have been entirely smothered, has at last produced fruit. And indeed no less seems to follow from the promise annexed to the command, "Train up a child in the way he should go, and when he is old he will not depart from it."

Having laid down these preliminaries, I shall say a few things upon the preservation of the health of children.

Perhaps you will think this belongs only to the physician: but though a physician ought to be employed to apply remedies in dangerous cases, any man, with a little reflection, may be allowed to form some judgment as to the ordinary means of their preservation; nay, I cannot help being of opinion, that any other man is fitter than a physician for this purpose. His thoughts are so constantly taken up with the rules of his art, that it is an hundred to one he will prescribe more methods and medicines than can be used with safety.

The fundamental rules for preserving the health of children, are cleanliness, liberty, and free air. By cleanliness I do not mean keeping the outside of their clothes in a proper condition to be seen before company, nor hindering them from fouling their hands and feet when they are capable of going abroad, but keeping them dry in the night-time, when young, and frequently washing their bodies with cold water, and other things of the same nature and tendency. The second rule is liberty: All persons, young and old, love liberty; and, as far as it does them no harm, it will certainly do them good. Many a free-born subject is kept a slave for the first ten years of his life, and is so much handled, and carried about by women in his infancy, that the limbs and other parts of his body are frequently misshapen, and the whole very much weakened; besides, the spirits, when under confinement, are generally in a dull and languishing state. The best exercise in the world for children, is to let them romp and jump about as soon as they are able, according to their own fancy. This, in the country, is best done in the fields; in a city, a well aired room is better than being sent into the streets under the care of a servant; very few of whom are able so far to curb their own inclinations, as to let the children follow theirs, even where they may do it with safety. As to free air, there is nothing more essentially necessary to the strength and growth of animals and plants. If a few plants of any kind are sown in a close confined place, they commonly grow up tall, small, and very weak. I have seen a bed of beans in a garden, under the shade of a hedge or tree, very long and slender, which brought to my mind a young family of quality, trained up in a delicate manner, who, if they grow at all, grow to length, but never to thickness. So universal is this, that I believe the body of a sturdy or well-built make, is reckoned among them a coarse and vulgar thing.

There is one thing, with regard to servants, that I would particularly recommend to your attention. All children are liable to accidents; these may happen unavoidably, but do generally arise from the carelessness of servants; and to this they are almost always attributed by parents. This disposes all servants, good or bad, to conceal them from the parents, when they can possibly do it. By this means children often receive hurts in falls or otherwise, which, if known in time, might be easily remedied, but not being known, either prove fatal, or make them lame or deformed. A near relation of mine has a high shoulder and a distorted waist, from this very cause. To prevent such accidents, it is necessary to take all pains possible to acquire the confidence of servants, to convince them of the necessity of concealing nothing. There are two dispositions in parents, which hinder the servants from making discoveries; the first is, when they are very passionate, and apt to storm and rage against their servants, for every real or supposed neglect. Such persons can never expect a confession, which must be followed by such terrible vengeance. The other is, when they are tender-hearted or timorous to excess; which makes them shew themselves deeply affected, or greatly terrified, upon any little accident that befalls their children. In this case, the very best servants are unwilling to tell them through fear of making them miserable. In such cases, therefore, I would advise parents, whatever may be their real opinion, to discover them as little as possible to their servants. Let them still inculcate this maxim, that there should be no secrets concerning children kept from those most nearly interested in them. And that there may be no temptation to such conduct, let them always appear as cool and composed as possible when any discovery is made, and be ready to forgive a real fault, in return for a candid acknowledgment.

LETTER II

IF I mistake not, my last letter was concluded by some remarks on the means of trying servants to be careful of the safety of children, and ready to discover, early and honestly, any accidents that might happen to befall them. I must make some farther remarks upon servants. It is a subject of great importance, and inseparably connected with what I have undertaken. You will find it extremely difficult to educate children properly, if the servants of the family do not conspire in it; and impossible, if they are inclined to hinder it. In such a case, the orders issued, or the method laid down, will be neglected, where that is possible and safe; where neglect is unsafe, they will be unsuccessfully or improperly executed, and many times, in the hearing of the children, they will be either laughed at, or complained of and disapproved. The certain consequence of this is, that children will insensibly come to look upon the directions and cautions of their parents, as unnecessary or unreasonable restraints. It is a known and very common way for servants to insinuate themselves into the affections of children, by granting them such indulgencies as would be refused them by their parents, as well as concealing the faults which ought to be punished by parents, and they are often very successful in training them up to a most dangerous fidelity in keeping the secret.

Such is the evil to be feared, which ought to have been more largely described; let us now come to the remedy. The foundation, to be sure, is to be very nice and careful in the choice of servants. This is commonly thought to be an extremely difficult matter, and we read frequently in the public papers, the heaviest complaints of bad servants. I am, however, one of those who think the fault is at least as often in the masters. Good servants may certainly be had, and do

generally incline of themselves to be in good families, and
when they find that they are so, do often continue very long
in the same, without desiring to remove. You ought, therefore, to be exceedingly scrupulous, and not without an evident necessity to hire any servant but who seems to be sober
and pious. Indeed I flatter myself, that a pious family is such
as none but one who is either a saint or a hypocrite will be
supposed to continue in. If any symptoms of the last character appear, you need not be told what you ought to do.

The next thing after the choice of servants, is to make
conscience of doing your duty to them, by example, instruction, admonition and prayer. Your fidelity to them will
naturally produce in them fidelity to you and yours, and that
upon the very best principles. It will excite in them a deep
sense of gratitude, and at the same time fill them with sentiments of the highest and most unfeigned esteem. I could tell
you of instances (you will however probably recollect some
yourself) of servants who, from their living comfortably and
receiving benefits in pious families, have preserved such a
regard and attachment to their masters, as have been little
short of idolatry. I shall just mention one—a worthy woman
in this place, formerly servant to one of my predecessors, and
married many years since to a thriving tradesman, continues
to have such an undiminished regard to her master's memory,
that she cannot speak of him without delight; keeps by her to
this hour the newspaper which gives an account of his death
and character, and, I believe, would not exchange it for a bill
or bond for a very considerable sum.

But the third and finishing direction with regard to servants, is to convince them, in a cool and dispassionate manner, of the reasonableness of your method of proceeding, that
as it is dictated by conscience, it is conducted with prudence.
Thence it is easy to represent to them that it is their duty,
instead of hindering its success by opposition or negligence,
to co-operate with it to the utmost of their power. It is not
below any man to reason in some cases with his servants.
There is a way of speaking to them on such subjects, by

which you will lose nothing of your dignity, but even corroborate your authority. While you manifest your firm resolution never to depart from your right and title to command, you may, notwithstanding, at proper seasons, and by way of condescension, give such general reasons for your conduct, as to shew that you are not acting by mere caprice or humour. Nay, even while you sometimes insist that your command of itself shall be a law, and that you will not suffer it to be disputed, nor be obliged to give a reason for it, you may easily shew them that this also is reasonable. They may be told that you have the greatest interest in the welfare of your children, the best opportunity of being apprised as to the means of prosecuting it, and that there may be many reasons for your orders, which it is unnecessary or improper for them to know.

Do not think that all this is excessive refinement, chimerical or impossible. Servants are reasonable creatures, and are best governed by a mixture of authority and reason. They are generally delighted to find themselves treated as reasonable, and will sometimes discover a pride in shewing that they understand, as well as find a pleasure in entering into your views. When they find, as they will every day by experience, the success and benefit of a proper method of education, it will give them a high opinion of, and confidence in your judgment; they will frequently consult you in their own affairs, as well as implicitly follow your directions in the management of yours. After all, the very highest instance of true greatness of mind, and the best support of your authority, when you see necessary to interpose it, is not to be opinionative or obstinate, but willing to acknowledge or remit a real mistake, if it is discreetly pointed out, even by those in the lower stations. The application of those reflections will occur in several of the following branches of this subject.

The next thing I shall mention as necessary, in order to the education of children, is, to establish as soon as possible an entire and absolute authority over them. This is a part of the subject which requires to be treated with great judgment and delicacy. I wish I may be able to do so. Opinions, like modes and fashions, change continually upon every point; neither is it easy to keep the just middle, without verging to one or other of the extremes. On this, in particular, we have gone in this nation in general, from one extreme, to the very utmost limits of the other. In the former age, both public and private, learned and religious education, was carried on by mere dint of authority. This, to be sure, was a savage and barbarous method, and was in many instances terrible and disgusting to the youth. Now, on the other hand, not only severity, but authority, is often decried; persuasion, and every soft and gentle method is recommended, on such terms as plainly lead to a relaxation. I hope you will be convinced that the middle way is best, when you find it is recommended by the Spirit of God in his word, Prov. xiii. 24. xix. 18. xxii. 15. You will also find a caution against excess in this matter, Col. ii. 21.

I have said above, that you should "establish, as soon as possible, an entire and absolute authority." I would have it early, that it may be absolute, and absolute, that it may not be severe. If parents are too long in beginning to exert their authority, they will find the task very difficult. Children, habituated to indulgence for a few of their first years, are exceedingly impatient of restraint; and if they happen to be of stiff or obstinate tempers, can hardly be brought to an entire, at least to a quiet and placid submission; whereas, if they are taken in time, there is hardly any temper but what may be made to yield, and by early habit the subjection becomes quite easy to themselves.

The authority ought also to be absolute, that it may not be severe. The more complete and uniform a parent's authority is, the offences will be more rare, punishment will be less needed, and the more gentle kind of correction will be abundantly sufficient. We see every where about us examples of this. A parent that has once obtained, and knows how to preserve authority, will do more by a look of displeasure, than another by the most passionate words, and even blows. It holds universally in families and schools, and even the greater bodies of men, the army and navy, that those who keep the strictest discipline give the fewest strokes. I have frequently remarked that parents, even of the softest tempers, and who are famed for the greatest indulgence to their children, do, notwithstanding, correct them more frequently, and even more severely, though to very little purpose, than those who keep up their authority. The reason is plain. Children, by foolish indulgence, become often so forward and petulant in their tempers that they provoke their easy parents past all endurance, so that they are obliged, if not to strike, at least to scold them, in a manner as little to their own credit as their childrens profit.

There is not a more disgusting sight, than the impotent rage of a parent who has no authority. Among the lower ranks of people, who are under no restraint from decency, you may sometimes see a father or mother running out into the street after a child who is fled from them, with looks of fury and words of execration, and they are often stupid enough to imagine, that neighbors or passengers will approve them in this conduct, though in fact it fills every beholder with horror. There is a degree of the same fault to be seen in persons of better rank, though expressing itself somewhat differently. Ill words and altercations will often fall out between parents and children before company; a sure sign that there is defect of government at home or in private. The parent, stung with shame at the misbehaviour or indiscretion of the child, desires to persuade the observers that it is not his fault, and thereby effectually convinces every person of reflection that it *is*.

I would therefore recommend to every parent to begin the establishment of authority much more early than is commonly supposed to be possible; that is to say, from about the age of eight or nine months. You will perhaps smile at this; but I do assure you from experience, that by setting about it with prudence, deliberation, and attention, it may be in a manner completed by the age of twelve or fourteen months. Do not imagine I mean to bid you use the rod at that age; on the contrary, I mean to prevent the use of it in a great measure, and to point out a way by which children of sweet and easy tempers may be brought to such a habit of compliance, as never to need correction at all; and whatever their temper may be, so much less of this is sufficient than upon any other supposition. This is one of my favourite schemes; let me try to explain and recommend it.

Habits, in general, may be very early formed in children. An association of ideas is, as it were, the parent of habit. If, then, you can accustom your children to perceive, that your will must always prevail over theirs, when they are opposed, the thing is done, and they will submit to it without difficulty or regret. To bring this about, as soon as they begin to shew their inclination by desire or aversion, let single instances be chosen now and then (not too frequently) to contradict them. For example, if a child shews a desire to have any thing in his hand that he sees, or has any thing in his hand with which he is delighted, let the parent take it from him, and when he does so, let no consideration whatever make him restore it at that time. Then at a considerable interval, perhaps a whole day is little enough, especially at first, let the same thing be repeated. In the mean time, it must be carefully observed, that no attempt should be made to contradict the child in the intervals. Not the least appearance of opposition, if possible, should be found between the will of the parent and that of the child, except in those chosen cases when the parent must always prevail.

I think it necessary that those attempts should always be made and repeated at proper intervals by the same person. It is also better it should be by the father than the mother or any female attendant, because they will be necessarily obliged, in many cases, to do things displeasing to the child, as in dressing, washing, &c. which spoil the operation; neither is it necessary that they should interpose, for when once a full authority is established in one person, it can easily be communicated to others, as far as is proper. Remember, however, that mother or nurse should never presume to condole with the child, or shew any signs of displeasure at his being crossed; but, on the contrary, give every mark of approbation, and of their own submission to the same person.

This experiment, frequently repeated, will in a little time so perfectly habituate the child to yield to the parent whenever he interposes, that he will make no opposition. I can assure you from experience, having literally practiced this method myself, that I never had a child of twelve months old, but who would suffer me to take any thing from him or her, without the least mark of anger or dissatisfaction, while they would not suffer any other to do so without the bitterest complaints. You will early perceive how this is to be extended gradually and universally, from one thing to another, from contradicting to commanding them. But this, and several other remarks upon establishing and preserving authority, must be referred to another letter.

LETTER III

DEAR SIR,

THE theory laid down in my last letter for establishing an early and absolute authority over children, is of much greater moment than perhaps you will immediately apprehend. There is a great diversity in the temper and disposition of children, and no less in the penetration, prudence, and resolution of parents. From all these circumstances difficulties arise, which increase very fast as the work is delayed. Some children have naturally very stiff and obstinate tempers, and some have a certain pride, or if you please, greatness of mind, which makes them think it a mean thing to yield. This disposition is often greatly strengthened in those of high birth, by the ideas of their own dignity and importance, instilled into them from their mother's milk. I have known a boy not six years of age, who made it a point of honour not to cry when he was beat, even by his parents. Other children have so strong passions, or so great sensibility, that if they receive correction they will cry immoderately, and either be, or seem to be, affected to such a degree, as to endanger their health or life. Neither is it uncommon for the parents in such a case to give up the point, and if they do not ask pardon, at least they give very genuine marks of repentance and sorrow for what they have done.

I have said this is not uncommon; but I may rather ask you, whether you know any parents at all, who have so much prudence and firmness as not to be discouraged in the one case, or to relent in the other? At the same time it must always be remembered, that the correction is wholly lost which does not produce absolute submission. Perhaps I may say it is more than lost, because it will irritate instead of reforming them, and will instruct or perfect them in the art of overcoming their parents, which they will not fail to manifest on a future opportunity. It is surprising to think how early children will discover the weak side of their parents, and what ingenuity they will shew in obtaining their favour or avoiding their displeasure. I think I have observed a child in treaty or expostulation with a parent, discover more consummate policy at seven years of age, than the parent himself, even when attempting to cajole him with artful evasions and specious promises. On all these accounts, it must be a vast advantage that a habit of submission should be brought on so early, that even memory itself shall not be able to reach back to its beginning. Unless this is done, there are many cases in which, after the best management, the authority will be imperfect; and some in which any thing that deserves that name will be impossible. There are some families, not contemptible either in station or character, in which the parents are literally and properly obedient to their children, are forced to do things against their will, and chidden if they discover the least backwardness to comply. If you know none such, I am sure I do.

Let us now proceed to the best means of preserving authority, and the way in which it ought to be daily exercised. I will trace this to its very source. Whatever authority you exercise over either children or servants, or as a magistrate over other citizens, it ought to be dictated by conscience, and directed by a sense of duty. Passion or resentment ought to have as little place as possible; or rather, to speak properly, though few can boast of having arrived at full perfection, it ought to have no place at all. Reproof or correction given in a rage, is always considered by him to whom it is administered, as the effect of weakness in you; and therefore the demerit of the offence will be either wholly denied or soon forgotten. I have heard some parents often say, that they cannot correct their children unless they are angry; to whom I have usually answered, Then you ought not to correct them at all. Every one would be sensible, that for a magistrate to discover an intemperate rage in pronouncing sentence against a criminal, would be highly indecent. Ought not parents to punish their children in the same dispassionate manner? Ought they not to be at least equally concerned to discharge their duty in the best manner, in the one case as in the other?

He who would preserve his authority over his children, should be particularly watchful of his own conduct. You may as well pretend to force people to love what is not amiable, as to reverence what is not respectable. A decency of conduct, therefore, and dignity of deportment, is highly serviceable for the purpose we have now in view. Lest this, however, should be mistaken, I must put in a caution, that I do not mean to recommend keeping children at too great a distance, by an uniform sternness and severity of carriage. This, I think, is not necessary, even when they are young; and it may, to children of some tempers, be very hurtful when they are old. By and bye you shall receive from me a quite contrary direction. But by dignity of carriage, I mean parents showing themselves always cool and reasonable in their own conduct; prudent and cautious in their conversation with regard to the rest of mankind; not fretful or impatient, or passionately fond of their own peculiarities; and though gentle and affectionate to their children, yet avoiding levity in their presence. This, probably, is the meaning of the precept of the ancients, *Maxima debetur pueris reverentia*. I would have them cheerful, yet serene. In short, I would have their familiarity to be evidently an act of condenscension. Believe it, my dear Sir, that which begets esteem, will not fail to produce subjection.

That this may not be carried too far, I would recommend every expression of affection and kindness to children when it is safe; that is to say, when their behavior is such as to deserve it. There is no opposition at all between parental tenderness and parental authority. They are the best supports to each other. It is not only lawful, but will be of service, that parents should discover the greatest fondness for children in infancy, and make them perceive distinctly with how much pleasure they gratify all their innocent inclinations. This, however, must always be done when they are quiet, gentle, and submissive in their carriage. Some have found fault with giving them, for doing well, little rewards of sweet-meats and play-things, as tending to make them mercenary, and leading them to look upon the indulgence of appetite as the chief good. This, I apprehend, is rather refining too much; the great point is, that they be rewarded for doing good, and not for doing evil. When they are cross and froward, I would never buy peace, but force it. Nothing can be more weak and foolish, or more destructive of authority, than when children are noisy and in an ill-humour, to give them or promise them something to appease them. When the Roman emperors began to give pensions and subsidies to the northern nations to keep them quiet, a man might have foreseen, without the spirit of prophecy, who would be master in a little time. The case is exactly the same with children. They will soon avail themselves of this easiness in their parents, command favours instead of begging them and be insolent when they· should be grateful.

The same conduct ought to be uniformly preserved, as children advance in years and understanding. Let parents try to convince them how much they have their real interest at heart. Sometimes children will make a request, and receive a hasty or froward denial; yet, upon reflection, the thing appears not to be unreasonable, and finally it is granted; and, whether it be right or wrong, sometimes by the force of importunity it is extorted. If parents expect either gratitude or submission for favours so ungraciously bestowed, they will

find themselves egregiously mistaken. It is their duty to pros-
ecute, and it ought to be their comfort to see the happiness of
their children; and therefore they ought to lay it down as a
rule, never to give a sudden or hasty refusal; but when any
thing is proposed to them, consider deliberately and fully
whether it is proper; and after that, either grant it cheerfully,
or deny it firmly.

It is a noble support of authority, when it is really and
visibly directed to the most important end. My meaning in
this, I hope, is not obscure. The end I consider as most
important is, the glory of God in the eternal happiness and
salvation of children. Whoever believes in a future state,
whoever has a just sense of the importance of eternity to
himself, cannot fail to have a like concern for his offspring.
This should be his end, both in instruction and government;
and when it visibly appears that he is under the constraint of
conscience, and that either reproof or correction are the fruit
of sanctified love, it will give them irresistible force. I will tell
you here, with all the simplicity necessary in such a situation,
what I have often said in my course of pastoral visitation in
families, where there is in many cases, through want of judgment as well as want of principle, a great neglect of authority:
"Use your authority for God, and he will support it. Let it
always be seen that you are more displeased at sin than at
folly. What a shame is it, that if a child shall, through the
inattention and levity of youth, break a dish, or a pane of the
window, by which you may lose the value of a few pence, you
should storm and rage at him with the utmost fury, or perhaps
beat him with unmerciful severity; but if he tells a lie, or takes
the name of God in vain, or quarrels with his neighbours, he
shall easily obtain pardon; or perhaps, if he is reproved by
others, you will justify him, and take his part."

You cannot easily believe the weight that it gives to family
authority, when it appears visibly to proceed from a sense of
duty, and to be itself an act of obedience to God. This will
produce coolness and composure in the manner; it will direct
and enable a parent to mix every expression of heart felt

tenderness, with the most severe and needful reproofs. It will make it quite consistent to affirm, that the rod itself is an evidence of love, and that it is true of every pious parent on earth, what is said of our Father in heaven, "Whom the Lord loveth he chasteneth, and scourgeth every son whom he receiveth. If ye endure chastening, God dealeth with you as with sons; for what son is he whom the Father chasteneth not? But if ye are without chastisement, whereof all are partakers, then ye are bastards and not sons." With this maxim in your eye, I would recommend, that solemnity take the place of, and be substituted for severity. When a child, for example, discovers a very depraved disposition, instead of multiplying stripes in proportion to the reiterated provocations, every circumstance should be introduced, whether in reproof or punishment, that can either discover the seriousness of your mind, or make an impression of awe and reverence upon his. The time may be fixed beforehand—at some distance—the Lord's day—his own birth-day—with many other circumstances that may be so special that it is impossible to enumerate them. I shall just repeat what you have heard often from me in conversation, that several pious persons made it an invariable custom, as soon as their children could read, never to correct them but after they had read over all the passages of Scripture which command it, and generally accompanied it with prayer to God for his blessing. I know well with what ridicule this would be treated by many, if publicly mentioned; but that does not shake my judgment in the least, being fully convinced it is a most excellent method, and that it is impossible to blot from the minds of children, while they live upon earth, the impressions that are made by these means, or to abate the veneration they will retain for the parents who acted such a part.

Suffer me here to observe to you, that such a plan as the above requires judgment, reflection, and great attention in your whole conduct. Take heed that there be nothing admitted in the intervals that counteract it. Nothing is more destructive of authority than frequent disputes and chiding upon small matters. This is often more irksome to children than parents are aware of. It weakens their influence insensibly, and in time makes their opinion and judgment of little weight, if not wholly contemptible. As before I recommended dignity in your general conduct, so, in a particular manner, let the utmost care be taken not to render authority cheap, by too often interposing it. There is really too great a risk to be run in every such instance. If parents will be deciding directly, and censuring every moment, it is to be supposed they will be sometimes wrong, and when this evidently appears, it will take away from the credit of their opinion, and weaken their influence, even where it ought to prevail.

Upon the whole, to encourage you to chuse a wise plan, and to adhere to it with firmness, I can venture to assure you, that there is no doubt of your success. To subdue a youth after he has been long accustomed to indulgence, I take to be in all cases difficult, and in many impossible; but while the body is tender, to bring the mind to submission; to train up a child in the nurture and admonition of the Lord, I know is not impossible: and he who hath given the command, can scarcely fail to follow it with his blessing.

8. Crispus (Anonymous): *On the Education of Children* (1814)

This anonymous essay captures the essence of the Calvinist position on child rearing and education in the early 19th century. What does it reveal about the author's assumptions regarding human nature, Christian experience, and childhood? How does it compare with earlier writings by English and American commentators? How might such a method of education affect the personalities of evangelicals?

ON THE EDUCATION OF CHILDREN

COMPLAINT is very frequently made, that habits of obedience and decorous behavior are, at the present day, less
observable in children than they were in the days of our
fathers. Allowance should be made, no doubt, for the veneration which we are apt to pay to things which are past, the
best side of which is perhaps retained in recollection, and the
worst forgotten; but still I am inclined to think, that we, who
are now on the stage, have greatly relaxed, in respect of
education, from the judicious precision of our ancestors. The
dread of being austere has carried us very far towards the
opposite extreme. Lest we should be too rigid, we have become too remiss. It is the fashion of the times to be lenient,
loose, licentious; and parents, out of mere *parental affection,*
as they would term it, must give their children some portion
of that indulgence, which they allow themselves. But it is not
so much my intention to expatiate on the extent of the evil, as
to point out a few causes of its existence, and to suggest some
means for its removal.

The root and foundation of misconduct in children is human depravity; depravity in the parent, and depravity in the
child. This ought never to be overlooked, nor forgotten in any
of our systems of education; but should be perpetually kept in
view. Corrupt ourselves, we look with a more favorable eye
upon the faults of our children, and feel a reluctance in
conveying a censure to them, which will recoil upon ourselves. Men cannot readily abhor their own resemblance;
they will regard it with tenderness, if not with complacency;
they will palliate what they cannot entirely excuse, and but
feebly rebuke what they dare not wholly pass over without
notice. This is on the supposition that the evil is *really,*

From *The Panoplist, and Missionary Magazine,* Vol. X (September 1814),
pp. 393–403. (The editor is grateful to Peter G. Slater for bringing this
source to his attention in his Ph.D. dissertation, "Views of Children and of
Child Rearing during the Early National Period: A Study in the New England Intellect" [University of California at Berkeley, 1970]).

though dimly seen; but this is not one half of the mischief. Human depravity renders the subject of it blind, and callous; it makes him insensible of the disorder which is upon him, and deliriously fond of his dangerous condition. It is a mad disease which allows its victim but few lucid intervals; and the glimpses which he then has at his true situation, serve only, in general, to bring on a recurrence of his disorder. Others, too, languish around him under the pressure of the same complaint: but their example does not abate his own malady, but rather adds to its violence. Such being the case, how shall the parent correct the child for a fault, which he is not perceived to possess; or which, if perceived, is lightly estimated, and possibly approved? Even the best of parents have very inadequate conceptions of the extensive evil of sin; and those conceptions, inadequate as they are, are rendered still more vague and feeble, when applied to the tender objects of parental affection, The parent, indeed, sees his child conducting amiss; but then it is only a weakness deserving commiseration, rather than censure; a momentary impulse which could not be avoided, and which will readily cease with the occasion which produced it. But this infantile weakness, inconsiderable as it is deemed, soon becomes gigantic, and bids defiance to the puny efforts which may afterwards be made for its coercion. The truth is, the parent cannot, or will not, believe, that *his* child, *his* offspring, *his* darling, is naturally dead in trespasses and sins; that *his* nature is corrupt, and the imagination of *his* heart is evil, and that only, and continually. He does not consider with what abhorrence God beholds those actions which he himself looks upon with so much indulgence. He does not consider with what abhorrence God beholds *his* criminal indifference to the growing sinfulness of his offspring; nor the dreadful impiety of treating those sins as trifling imbecilities, which the Most High declares worthy of eternal punishment. Did the parent look upon sin as exceedingly sinful, he would not regard with indifference, and even with complacence, those strong indications of it, which every child exhibits, as soon as it begins to express its feelings at all.

But are children indeed so depraved from the birth; are they naturally so corrupt; that the parent's regarding their little foibles, and occasional sallies of harmless passion without any very strong disapprobation, is to be accounted sinful, and as affording evidence of his own depravity? Such, and similar, questions are often asked, and they amount to pretty strong evidence that the person, who asks them, is himself very far gone in depravity; or at least has been a very inattentive observer of his children's temper and disposition. We often hear parents calling their children "harmless creatures," "pretty innocents," and other fond and endearing names which *figuratively* denote the same thing, such as "little doves," "harmless birds," with a thousand other equivalent appellations; and, I confess, I never hear them without trembling, lest those, their unfledged offspring, should prove birds of evil omen, if not birds of prey, fitted to be taken themselves at last in the snare of the fowler. Take an infant yet unable to walk, and offend him. With every natural member of annoyance, which he is able to exert, he will give you proof palpable and positive, that he has other attributes than those which are purely innoxious. No sooner does a child begin to take notice of objects so as to be pleased with them, than he covets them; and no sooner does he covet, than he endeavors, by all means in his power, to possess them, not by gentle methods, but by force. Completely selfish, he admits no opposite rights, nor claims. His object is to gratify himself; and every thing in opposition to this is assaulted with violence, and the interference of others is treated with turbulent resentment. Persons many times wonder, that infants should come into the world, and continue a great length of time, weak and helpless, while the young of other creatures are either immediately, or within a very short period of time, strong and active. But surely a little reflection would teach us the goodness of God in this particular. Were infants from the birth endowed with strength and activity like the young of some animals, the most fatal effects would follow. Give the child the strength of manhood without abating ought from the violence and perverseness of his temper; who would willingly be his nurse, or his attendants? In such a case, instead of the present milder measures of restraint, you would be compelled, for your own safety, to resort to chains and fetters, and to invent new methods of coercion in order to reduce him to obedience. In his paroxisms of rage at some disappointment in his pleasures, would he hesitate, do you think, to take your life, were you the cause of his exasperation; or, failing in this attempt, would he scruple to lay violent hands on himself, or to do some other act of direful import? Did you never see a child in some fit of passion, who wanted nothing but the power to make such scenes real? And from what can such a disposition proceed, except from the most deep-rooted depravity? But this, you reply, is an extreme case, and cannot prove a generally depraved disposition, Does he not at other times sport and play; is he not pleased with my caresses; is he not attached to those by whom he is fed, and by whom he is fondled? Undoubtedly; and the depravity of his temper is, for this very reason, the more conspicuous. On these very objects of his affection that is, objects of affection, so long as they please him, it is, that on turning the tables, he will vent the utmost of his resentment. Offend him, and all past attachments and good offices are forgotten; his impotence, and not his gratitude, will prove his own restraint, and your protection. Offer him food which he does not want, or when he is sullen; will he be pleased with it, or will he thank you? Caress him when he is angry; will he return you *his* caresses, before he has gained his object, or until he has forgotten the cause of his anger? When he plays, is it to gratify another, or *himself?* Will he give up his play things before he is tired of them, in order that another may play with them? Or will he scruple to demand, and forcibly to take, another's play things, whether the latter has done with them or not? To prove a child's depravity, it cannot be necessary to show, that he is con-

stantly in a passion, that he is every moment a fury, which
nothing can withstand. Nor can any argument against his
depravity be derived from the fact, that he often plays, and
sports, and prattles. Were he incapable of pleasure, and of
expressing it, he would not be human. His depravity is always
ready to manifest itself, whenever there is an occasion to
draw it forth; and when there is no such occasion, the disposition is as really there, as if it were in exercise.

If, then, both parents and children are depraved, it becomes important that the former should be well aware, that
this moral distemper is upon them. They should not deceive
themselves in a matter of so much moment. The *fact* will
remain unaltered, whatever credit they may please to attach
to it; nor is their responsibility diminished, because they do
not choose to open their eyes to conviction. True wisdom
would teach them to adapt themselves to the real state of
things; to foresee the evil, and guard against it. Let the parent
be convinced, that he has in him a disposition to that which is
evil, and which, if not corrected, will lead him to ruin; he will
then the more readily believe that his children possess the
same disposition, and will feel the more strongly their need of
his parental guidance. Let him once obtain the mastery over
this disposition in himself, he will then the better understand
how to apply proper correctives to the same malady in his
children. Let him be very cautious how he indulges himself in
the very common fault of discrediting every thing which impeaches the innocence of his children; of imagining *his* children to be faultless. Let him take the fact as it is; let him
believe, feel, and acknowledge, that even *his* offspring, *his*
darlings, are naturally perverse; that they are by nature just
as bad as the children of other people; that they are possessed
of the same natural temper, have the same malignant passions, and that *their* faults are viewed with no greater complacency by the eye of Him, who can never be a respecter of
persons.

Some parents from a false affection for their children, have
always some sort of excuse ready at hand for every error

which they commit. The child is sick, is fatigued, is affrighted, is abused, is grieved, or is something else, which is sure to have no harm in it, whenever he manifests any ill humor. Though he should rave and storm like a maniac, still human corruption has no hand in it; some commonplace apology is made in his behalf; and the child, half smothered with caresses, is pronounced sweet-tempered as a lamb. Exactly in proportion as he is ill-natured, he is indulged; and the more indulgence he receives, the more he demands; till at length it becomes a question of no doubtful solution, which governs, the parent or the child? But let it be remembered, that every palliation of a fault gives countenance to it — is a premium set upon iniquity; and that no parent can offer such a premium and be guiltless. To his guidance and care are committed the interests of an immortal soul; he is deeply responsible for the trust. If he allows and fosters that which God abhors; if he calls that innocent and good, which God pronounces evil; and justifies that which God condemns, he opposes the divine constitution of right and wrong, and impeaches the veracity of the Most High. In such a controversy, whose decision shall stand? In such an issue, whose cause shall be maintained?

But to thwart and control the inclinations of children is cruel and unkind. Yet in what does this cruelty consist. To be cruel, is to inflict unnecessary pain. To confer a benefit, is to be kind. If your children possess dispositions that lead them into sin, it surely cannot be cruel to check those dispositions, or give them a new and better direction. It is very strange that Christian parents should deem it cruel and unkind, to refuse their children the *pleasures of sin;* for to this the indulgence of their perverse and froward tempers actually amounts. *They,* certainly, ought to know that all children, their own included in the number, have naturally corrupt passions and propensities; that such passions and propensities, without restraint, will certainly lead to sin; and sin conducts to endless ruin. *They,* certainly, ought to know, that the Most High regards whatever tends to sin with utter abhorrence, and that sin is that abominable thing which his soul hates. How then can *they* view with such complacency, what He regards with

indignation; or deem that as cruel, which saves their children
from the effect of His displeasure? Can they deem it an act of
unkindness to teach their children habits of obedience, both
to Divine and parental authority; and for this purpose to give
them lessons in self-denial in the ways of sin, or even to
compel them to cease to do evil, and to learn to do well? Is it
an act of unkindness to attempt to save a soul from death?
Yet such, let it be remembered, is the natural tendency of
parental discipline when properly directed. I do not say that it
will of itself infallibly produce this desirable effect; but certain
it is, that it tends that way, and that it serves to prevent their
progress in the opposite course, which leads to the chambers
of death. Here, then, are powerful motives to attempt the
proper government of children; motives which all parents,
and especially Christian parents, ought most sensibly to feel.
Yet strange as it may seem, many, who call themselves Christians, are, in these matters, as greatly delinquent, as the mere
people of the world; as prone to complain of the cruelty of
enforcing their commands on their offspring, and equally indulgent to their wayward caprices. Some, who make no pre-
tensions to religion, often excel this class of persons, in correct and wholesome discipline; more effectually restrain their
children from evil courses; better accustom them to useful
habits; and with more scrupulosity bar the avenues to sin and
ruin. But Christianity, if rightly understood and applied, ought
to insure, and will insure, a better education than mere moral-
ity, or a mere sense of propriety, can ever produce. When
those, therefore, who are styled Christians, fail to train up
their children to virtuous and useful habits, it is very apparent
that they neglect their trust, and poorly employ the talents
committed to their keeping. They wound the cause of religion, and lead the ungodly to say, if not actually to believe,
that religion tends to licentiousness, and presents less impos-
ing motives to obedience, than the maxims of mere human
prudence and invention.

But to insure, as far as may be, the proper behavior of his
children, let every parent make it his inflexible determination,
that he will be obeyed—*invariably* obeyed. An uniform adher-

ence to this resolution will save him from a multitude of difficulties, and produce incalculable good. The sum and substance of good government is to *be obeyed;* not now and then, when the humor suits; but always, and *invariably.* The child should know on what it has to depend, and should not be lost in uncertain conjectures, whether you really *intend* to be obeyed; whether you merely *propose* obedience, or actually *command* it. If you do not mean to enforce obedience, it ought not to be commanded; if you mean to command it, it ought to be enforced. The connexion between *your* command, and *his* obedience, should be as certain as that between cause and effect; the one should be the unfailing consequent of the other. It is hardly necessary to say, that your commands should respect things lawful and proper to be done; for surely unlawful commands have very little to do with good government. Your commands may indeed respect things previously indifferent; but the moment you command them they lose that character, and become positive duties, the performance of which is as indispensable, as your authority to enjoin them was proper and unquestionable. But you will ask, am I to whip and torture my children for every little infraction of my orders, and play the tyrant in order to enforce their obedience? A hard case surely—but one of your own making. Habitual obedience has no need of such severities; it is yielded readily, and as a matter of course. Nothing short of very obstinate and habitual disobedience can bring matters to such extremities. Parents, who govern well, never suffer their children to arrive at such a pass, that nothing short of torture will coerce them. They commence the business in season, and enforce obedience by gentler methods; they master the disease at its first appearance, and so avoid the necessity of desperate remedies. A moderate, but equable, regimen afterwards succeeds; such as is calculated to prevent relapses, and to invigorate the system. It is worthy of observation that parents, who govern badly, usually correct their children most; and how should it be otherwise? If children are not taught to obey habitually, how can obedience be expected from them occasionally, without resort to compulsory measures. The child that is accustomed to disobey in nine cases out of ten, will always remember that the chance of escaping punishment is in his favor, and nothing short of actual smarting will suffice to convince him that obedience is really demanded. The truth is, children always learn to obey, at first, from a sense of necessity, not from a sense of moral duty. If they consider this necessity to be uniform, their obedience will be so; if the necessity be only occasional, such also will be their obedience. Hence it happens, that those parents who suffer their children to disobey them generally with impunity, find themselves really obliged to resort to severe methods, in order to enforce their commands.

I am no friend to frequent and severe punishment; I neither consider it necessary, nor an evidence of proper discipline. But to abstain wholly from correction, except in some extraordinary cases, when probably both parent and child are extremely exasperated, affords surely no proof of suitable parental affection. It may, however, prove one point, that this parental *tenderness,* so much extolled, can be dispensed with, when the gratification of other passions comes into competition; while it affords little evidence of any great progress in the art of self-government.

But says one, I too am of opinion that it does no good to chastise children perpetually: the little *things,* as they grow in years, will grow in discretion, and will of themselves soon learn to lay aside improper habits, and to conduct correctly. I never use the rod: when they arrive at a proper age, I endeavor to *reason* them into their duty. My feelings are too tender to suffer *my* children to be put to unnecessary pain.

This very *sensitive* parent must permit me to ask him one or two questions. Is it out of regard to *yourself,* or to your *child,* to save *yourself* or *him,* from pain, that you never chastise him? Is it not more from a regard to your own feelings, than to his good, that you are so very lenient, in a plain case of duty? Are you willing to have the *trouble* of doing your duty to your children? Have you not some whim, some prejudice, some conceit, of which you are, in reality, more tender, than you are of your children's welfare? To be frank, my own opinion is, that almost all the excuses which parents make to cover their neglect of training up their children to obedience, have their origin in sheer selfishness; in their own self-gratification and caprice, more than in any real tenderness towards those objects of their indulgence; and that they in fact prefer their own humors to their children's welfare.

But what says Divine truth on the subject of correcting children? The Spirit of inspiration, surely has given no improper directions on this topic; nor can their Heavenly Parent be supposed to have a less tender and suitable regard to his children, than have their earthly ones. By consulting the Scriptures, we shall find that those parents do not best consult their children's welfare, who withhold correction from them, when they forsake their duty. *He that spareth his rod, hateth his son; but he that loveth him, chasteneth him betimes.* He begins in season, and repeats the chastening so often as there is occasion; and this, instead of showing that he has no affection for his son, proves that he loves him. *Foolishness is bound in the heart of a child; but the rod of correction shall drive it from him. Withhold not correction from the child, for if thou beatest him with a rod, he shall not die.* A very different sentiment from one often peevishly intimated — *shall I kill my child to make him obey me?* It is believed, however, that few children *die in that way. — The rod and reproof give wisdom; but a child left to himself, bringeth his mother to shame.* Another sentiment altogether opposed to one very prevalent among parents, that discipline makes a child dumpish and stupid, impairs his mental faculties, and oppresses his animal spirits. But it seems that the plainest declarations of Scripture are to pass for nothing, provided our criminal negligence can find a covering. Many affect to believe that a child left to himself will bring his parents to honor; will grow up a man of spirit, superior to low and vulgar prejudices. The experience of all ages, however, proves them to be mistaken, and that in this case, as well as in others, *God is true,* and men, when opposed to him, *are liars.* So true is it that a *a child left to himself bringeth his mother,* in other words, *his parents* to shame; that such a child always carries with him the badge of his own and their disgrace. His want of subordination betrays itself in every successive stage of life; at home and abroad; in his boyish pastimes, and in the pursuits of manhood; in private, and in public relations. How common is it to remark, that such an one shows his *bringing up;* that he betrays his *breeding;* that he learned his bad habits *at home;* and to conclude with saying, it is no wonder, for his parents always *indulged him.* Such remarks are not made directly to the parents themselves; *they,* in the mean while, are congratulating themselves secretly, and perhaps publicly, on their superior wisdom in managing, or rather *not* managing their children; idolizing them in imagination, at the expense of their fellows. No fault is told a person with more reluctance, than that he fails in family government; hence he commonly continues ignorant of his mistake, till some flagrant misconduct convinces him of it, and he is usually brought to shame at a time, and in a manner, which he had least expected, and while priding himself, that his children thus left to themselves would bring him to honor. Again, it is commanded; *Chasten thy son while there is hope, and let not thy soul spare for his crying.* That is, defer not this duty until it shall be too late, nor let false compassion keep you from its performance. It is here worthy of remark, that an Apostle teaches Christians to infer, from the chastisements which they receive, that they are the children of God, in the same manner, and for the same reason, as they would infer, that a child which received correction from an earthly parent, was not illegitimate. *If ye endure chastening, God dealeth with you as with sons: for what son is he whom the father chasteneth not. But if ye be without chastisement, whereof all are partakers, then are ye bastards, and not sons.* But how many children are there among us at this day, who from the want of proper chastisement, are more like illegitimate than acknowledged sons; who grow up as untutored as do those unfortunate beings alluded to, cast off from the birth, unacknowledged, groping into manhood without a guide, and without a helper! Need parents to be exhorted to rescue themselves and their children from the imputation of such disgrace?

Let it be admitted, then, that children ought to be trained to obedience, and, if necessary, to receive chastisement: at what age shall parental authority be exerted for this purpose? I answer, there is little danger of its being exerted too soon; the danger is altogether on the other side. I know not that a child was ever injured by commencing the habit of obedience too young; very many have been ruined by neglecting it till too late. A child will learn either to obey, or disobey; there is no middle ground. If he learns the first, you have your desire, and your subsequent task to continue the habit will be comparatively light. First impressions ought to be good; they are easiest made, and usually strong and abiding. But if the child first acquires the habit of disobeying, you have then not only to teach him a new habit afterwards, but have also an old one to obliterate; and you need not be told how much easier it is to establish, than to destroy, a habit. If a child is taught to obey, and knows of no way to avoid it, he will obey of course, and do it cheerfully. If you compel him only now and then to listen to your commands, and suffer him at other times to do as he pleases, he will obey you only from compulsion, and never from habit. But in beginning to establish your authority over him, it is advisable that your first commands should be of the negative kind. Order him *not to do* a thing, rather than *to do it*. You can more easily compel him to *desist* from an action, than to perform one; and in that way you establish your authority to the full as well, for you teach him to obey, and that is the whole which you have in view. When once taught to obey your negative commands, he will readily submit to such as are positive. I have known parents spend more time, use severer measures, and put their children to more pain, in endeavoring to procure their submission to one single positive command, and give up the point at last, than would have been necessary to secure their obedience for life, had the business been undertaken in season, and conducted properly afterwards. It is unnecessary, perhaps impossible, to assign any precise age, at which this work of obedience is to be commenced. It is sufficient to say, that as soon as a child is old enough to form wishes that ought not to be gratified, to be malignant, obstinate and turbulent, if he is crossed in obtaining them, it is time to deny him the gratification of his desires, and to restrain his resentment which may in consequence ensue. If he is old enough to be spiteful, and vindictive, when you interfere with the objects which he covets, it is time that you teach him self-denial, and reduce him to a better temper. Here begin; here interpose your parental authority; accustom him to be denied, and to take it patiently; habituate him to submit *his* will to *yours,* and to take pleasure in gratifying *you,* as well as *himself.* My own opinion is, that by the time a child is two years old, the important work of securing his obedience may and ought to be accomplished; oftentimes still earlier; and that the business is better and more effectually done then, than at a later period. It was the advice of the late President Witherspoon, that sagacious observer of human nature and truly great man, to begin with the infant, as soon as he should manifest a fondness for a play thing, and, before he should obstinately covet it, to take it from him, and so gradually habituate him to self-denial, and to his parent's authority. It was his opinion that in this way, the child might be taught the habit of obedience without punishment, and without a contest. I have known the experiment to be made in part, and so far with entire success. But on this particular topic, and the subject of education generally, I cannot do so well as to refer my readers to the author himself in his "Letters on Education;" a work which every parent ought to read, and which contains more practical good sense on the subject in hand, than I remember to have seen in any other book, the Bible excepted.

Many parents will not hesitate to acknowledge themselves

culpable in neglecting the proper discipline of their children. The task, they say, is difficult, and one to which they are not equal; their will is good, but their resolution feeble. Having said this, they seem to feel as if they had disburdened their consciences by so frank a confession, and then very quietly pursue the same path which they had previously trodden. But in such a case, something more is required than empty confessions of allowed faults, to remedy the mischief which they have occasioned. If they have erred, this furnishes no reason for continuing the error, but a very strong one for relinquishing it. Nor is proper discipline so difficult a task as it is represented. The real difficulties lie on the other side; the object of discipline is to avoid, not to create them. Who meets with most difficulties; the parent that has his children under due subordination, or he that suffers them to live without any control? But allow the task to be as difficult as it is represented; are you unwilling to encounter a few obstacles for the sake of your children? Had you rather ruin them by your neglect, than promote their best interests at the expense of a pittance of your present ease? Is a plain and obvious duty to be abandoned, because some trifling obstacle may oppose its fulfillment? The truth is, great numbers of our countrymen have gone very far in the neglect of parental discipline, and are more willing to acknowledge or palliate the fault, than they are to renounce it. Every one can *talk* on the subject, as it happens to strike his humor at the moment; can condemn, or justify himself as circumstances vary, or the occasion suits him. But without serious pains to produce a reformation, the evil has taken too deep root to be easily eradicated. The united efforts of all, who rightly estimate the importance of obedience to parents, are necessary to arrest the progress of the mischief complained of, and to restore us to that better course, which our fathers took in training up their children for public and private usefulness. In the number of those against whom, the Apostle tells us, the wrath of God is revealed from Heaven, are the *disobedient to parents,* and such as are *without natural affection.* At the present day too many can be found who answer to this description. A multitude of parents daily contribute to the revelation of this wrath, by their neglect in educating their children to obedience; herein manifesting their own want of proper natural affection, and teaching them also the same impiety. Had we our choice, with which generation should we wish to have our lot; with such an one as lived fifty years ago, or such, as from present prospects, without a special interposition of Providence, is like to be on the stage of action at the end of half a century to come? May our efforts be such, and such be the blessing attendant upon them, that future generations may account themselves happy in being descended from those, who put a just value on faithful parental discipline, and filial obedience.

CRISPUS

9. John S. C. Abbott:
On the Mother's Role in Education (1833)

Although born in Brunswick, Maine, in 1805, John Stevens Cabot Abbott was a descendant of Puritan ancestors who settled in Andover, Massachusetts, in the 1630's. For generations, the Abbots of Andover had been active members of the South Parish Congregational Church, successfully perpetuating many of the beliefs and much of the piety of the family founders through the 18th and into the 19th century. Thus, when John S. C. Abbott graduated from the Andover Theological Seminary and became a Congregationalist minister, he was maintaining a traditional commitment of his family to the ancient New England way. He served as pastor in five different churches in Massachusetts and Connecticut during the course of his life and wrote more than 50 books on historical and religious subjects, but his fame rested most on his first book, *The Mother at Home*. Important both for its exaltation of the role of motherhood in the family and its practical advice on child-rearing methods, Abbott's book epitomised the moderated views of early 19th-century evangelicals.

PREFACE

THE object of this book is *practical utility,* not literary effect. It was written for mothers in the common walks of life. There are many mothers, in every village of our land, who are looking eagerly for information respecting the government of their children. It is hoped that the following treatise may render them some assistance.

Some persons may object to the minuteness of detail, and the familiarity of illustration, occasionally introduced. We, however, are persuaded that this objection will not be made by *mothers.* Education consists in attention to *little things.*

The religious sentiments inculcated in this book are those usually denominated *evangelical.* We have proceeded upon the principle that here is the commencement of eternal existence, and that the great object of education is to prepare the child for its heavenly home.

When a person writes upon the subject of family government, the first thought which arises in the minds of many readers, is, "we will see how he succeeds in his own family." There are many motives, such as indolence, false tenderness, &c. operating to induce a parent to neglect known duty. The principles contained in this book may be correct, even though the author should fail to enforce them.

This treatise was commenced with particular reference to the mothers who attend my ministry. That it may be of assistance to them, in their efforts to lead their children to the Savior, is the earnest prayer of their friend and pastor,

JOHN S. C. ABBOTT

THE MOTHER AT HOME

CHAPTER I.   RESPONSIBILITY

A FEW years ago, some gentlemen who were associated in preparing for the ministry, felt interested in ascertaining what proportion of their number had pious mothers. They were greatly surprised and delighted in finding that out of one hundred and twenty students, over a hundred had been borne by a mother's prayers, and directed by a mother's counsels, to the Savior. Though some of these had broken away from all the restraints of home, and like the prodigal, had wandered in sin and sorrow, yet they could not forget the impressions of childhood, and were eventually brought to the Savior, to be a mother's joy and blessing. Many interesting facts have, within a few years, drawn the attention of Christians to this subject. The efforts which a mother makes for the improvement of her child in knowledge and virtue, are necessarily retired and unobtrusive. The world knows not of them; and hence the world has been slow to perceive how powerful and extensive is this secret and silent influence. But circumstances are now directing the eyes of the community to the nursery, and the truth is daily coming more distinctly before the public, that the influence which is exerted upon the mind during the first eight or ten years of existence, in a great degree guides the destinies of that mind for time and eternity. And as the mother is the guardian and guide of the early years of life, from her goes the most powerful influence in the formation of the character of man. And why should it not be so? What impressions can be more strong, and more lasting, than those received upon the mind in the freshness and the susceptibility of youth? What instructor can gain greater confidence and respect than a mother? And where can there be delight in

---

From John S. C. Abbott, *The Mother at Home; or the Principles of Maternal Duty Familiarly Illustrated* (New York: The American Tract Society, 1833), pp. 5-6, 9-14, 22-25, 27-29, 38-41, 45, 51, 59-64, 116-119, 150-153, 159-161.

acquiring knowledge, if not when the little flock cluster around a mother's knee to hear of God and heaven?

"A good boy generally makes a good man." Said the mother of Washington, "George was always a good boy." Here we see one secret of his greatness. George Washington had a mother who made him a good boy, and instilled into his heart those principles which raised him to be the benefactor of his country, and one of the brightest ornaments of the world. The *mother* of Washington is entitled to a nation's gratitude. *She* taught her boy the principles of obedience, and moral courage, and virtue. She, in a great measure, formed the character of the hero, and the statesman. It was by her own fire-side that she taught her playful boy to govern himself; and thus was he prepared for the brilliant career of usefulness which he afterward pursued. We are indebted to God for the gift of Washington; but we are no less indebted to him for the gift of his inestimable mother. Had she been a weak, and indulgent, and unfaithful parent, the unchecked energies of Washington might have elevated him to the throne of a tyrant; or youthful disobedience might have prepared the way for a life of crime and a dishonored grave.

Byron had a mother just the reverse of lady Washington; and the character of the mother was transferred to the son. We cannot wonder then at his character and conduct, for we see them to be the almost necessary consequence of the education he received, and the scenes witnessed in his mother's parlor. She would at one time allow him to disobey with impunity; again she would fly into a rage and beat him. She thus taught him to defy all authority, human and divine; to indulge, without restraint, in sin; to give himself up to the power of every maddening passion. It was the mother of Byron who laid the foundation of his pre-eminence in guilt. She taught him to plunge into that sea of profligacy and wretchedness, upon whose agitated waves he was tossed for life. If the crimes of the poet deserve the execration of the world—the world cannot forget that it was the mother who fostered in his youthful heart those passions which made the son a curse to his fellow-men.

There are, it is true, innumerable causes incessantly operating in the formation of character. A mother's influence is by no means the only influence which is exerted. Still it may be the most powerful; for, with God's ordinary blessing, it may form in the youthful mind the habits, and implant the principles, to which other influences are to give permanency and vigor.

A pious and faithful mother *may have* a dissolute child. He may break away from all restraints, and God may leave him to "eat the fruit of his own devices." The parent, thus afflicted and broken-hearted, can only bow before the sovereignty of her Maker, who says, "be still, and know that I am God." The consciousness, however, of having done one's duty, divests this affliction of much of its bitterness. And besides, such cases are rare. Profligate children are generally the offspring of parents who have neglected the moral and religious education of their family. Some parents are themselves profligate, and thus not only allow their children to grow up unrestrained, but by their example lure them to sin. But there are others, who are very upright, and virtuous, and even pious themselves, who do, nevertheless, neglect the moral culture of their children; and as a consequence, they grow up in disobedience and sin. It matters but little what the cause is which leads to this neglect. The neglect itself will ordinarily be followed by disobedience and self-will.

Hence the reason that children of eminent men, both in church and state, are not unfrequently the disgrace of their parents. If the mother is unaccustomed to govern her children, if she look to the father to enforce obedience, and to control; when *he* is absent, all family government is absent, and the children are left to run wild; to learn lessons of disobedience; to practise arts of deception; to build, upon the foundation of contempt for a mother, a character of insubordination and iniquity. But if the children are under the efficient government of a judicious mother, the reverse of this is almost invariably the case. And since, in nearly every instance, the early years of life are intrusted to a mother's care, it follows that maternal influence, more than any thing else, forms the future character.

• • • • •

You have watched over your child, through all the months of its helpless infancy. You have denied yourself, that you might give it comfort. When it has been sick, you have been unmindful of your own weariness, and your own weakness, and the livelong night you have watched at its cradle, administering to all its wants. When it has smiled, you have felt a joy which none but a parent can feel, and have pressed your much loved treasure to your bosom, praying that its future years of obedience and affection might be your ample reward. And now, how dreadful a requital, for that child to grow up to hate and abuse you; to leave you friendless, in sickness and in poverty; to squander all his earnings in haunts of iniquity and degradation.

How entirely is your earthly happiness at the disposal of your child! His character is now, in an important sense, in your hands, and you are to form it for good or for evil. If you are consistent in your government, and faithful in the discharge of your duties, your child will probably through life revere you, and be the stay and solace of your declining years. If, on the other hand, you cannot summon resolution to punish your child when disobedient; if you do not curb his passions; if you do not bring him to entire and willing subjection to your authority; you must expect that he will be your curse. In all probability, he will despise you for your weakness. Unaccustomed to restraints at home, he will break away from all restraints, and make you wretched by his life, and disgraceful in his death.

But few parents think of this as they ought. They are not conscious of the tremendous consequences dependent upon the efficient and decisive government of their children. Thousands of parents now stand in our land like oaks blighted and scathed by lightnings and storms. Thousands have had every hope wrecked, every prospect darkened, and have become the victims of the most agonizing and heart-rending disappointment, solely in consequence of the misconduct of their children. And yet thousands of others are going on in the same way, preparing to experience the same suffering, and are apparently unconscious of their danger.

It is true that there are many mothers who feel their responsibilities perhaps as deeply as it is best they should feel them. But there are many others — even of Christian mothers — who seem to forget that their children will ever be less under their control than they are while young. And they are training them up, by indecision and indulgence, soon to tyrannize over their parents with a rod of iron — and to pierce their hearts with many sorrows. If you are unfaithful to your child when he is young, he will be unfaithful to you when he is old. If you indulge him in all his foolish and unreasonable wishes when he is a child, when he becomes a man he will indulge himself; he will gratify every desire of his heart; and your sufferings will be rendered the more poignant by the reflection that it was your own unfaithfulness which has caused your ruin. If you would be the happy mother of a happy child, give your attention, and your efforts, and your prayers, to the great duty of training him up for God and heaven.

CHAPTER II. MATERNAL AUTHORITY

I HAVE thus endeavored to show the mother how much her happiness is dependant upon the good or bad character of her children. Your own reflections and observation have, doubtless, impressed this subject most deeply upon your heart. The question has probably often presented itself to your mind, while reading the previous chapter, "How shall I govern my children, so as to secure their virtue and happiness?" This question I shall now endeavor to answer.

1. *Obedience* is absolutely essential to proper family gov-

ernment. Without this, all other efforts will be in vain. You may pray with, and for your children; you may strive to instruct them in religious truth; you may be unwearied in your efforts to make them happy, and to gain their affection. But if they are in habits of disobedience, your instructions will be lost, and your toil in vain. And by *obedience,* I do not mean languid and dilatory yielding to repeated threats, but prompt and cheerful acquiescence in parental commands. Neither is it enough that a child should yield to your *arguments* and *persuasions.* It is essential that he should submit to your authority.

· · · · ·

It is certainly the duty of parents to convince their children of the reasonableness and propriety of their requirements. This should be done to instruct them, and to make them acquainted with moral obligation. But there should always be *authority* sufficient to enforce prompt obedience, whether the child can see the reason of the requirement or not. Indeed, it is impossible to govern a child by mere argument. Many cases must occur, in which it will be incapable of seeing the reasonableness of the command; and often its wishes will be so strongly opposed to duty, that all the efforts to convince will be in vain. The first thing therefore, to be aimed at, is to bring your child under perfect subjection. Teach him that he must obey you. Sometimes give him your reasons; again withhold them. But let him perfectly understand that he is to do as he is bid. Accustom him to immediate and cheerful acquiescence in your will. This is obedience. And this is absolutely essential to good family government. Without this, your family will present one continued scene of noise and confusion; the toil of rearing up your children will be almost insupportable, and, in all probability, your heart will be broken by their future licentiousness or ingratitude.

II. We come now to the inquiry, *how is this habit of obedience to be established?* This is not so difficult a matter as many imagine. It does not require profound learning, or a mysterious skill, which pertains but to the few. Where do you find the best regulated families? Are they in the houses of the rich? Do the children of our most eminent men furnish the best patterns for imitation? Obviously not. In some of the most humble dwellings we find the beautiful spectacle of an orderly and well regulated family. On the other hand, in the mansions of the wealthiest or most eminent men of our country, we may often find a family of rude girls and ungovernable boys, — a picture of wild misrule. It is not greatness of talent, or profound learning, which is requisite to teach a child obedience. The principles by which we are to be guided are very simple and very plain.

Never give a command which you do not intend shall be obeyed.

There is no more effectual way of teaching a child disobedience, than by giving commands which you have no intention of enforcing. A child is thus habituated to disregard its mother; and in a short time the habit becomes so strong, and the child's contempt for the mother so confirmed, that entreaties and threats are alike unheeded.

• • • • •

Is it said that by noticing such *little things* a mother must be continually finding fault? But it is not a *little thing* for a child to disobey a mother's commands. This one act of disregarding authority prepares the way for another. It is the commencement of evil which must be resisted. The very first appearances of insubordination must be checked. There are doubtless cases of trifling faults occurring, which a wise parent will judge it expedient to overlook. Children will be thoughtless and inadvertent. They will occasionally err from strict propriety, without any real intention of doing wrong. Judgment is here requisite in deciding what things must be overlooked; but we may be assured, I think, that direct and open disobedience is not, in any case, to be classed among

the number of trifling faults. The eating of an apple banished
our first parents from paradise. The atrocity of the offence
consisted in its *disobedience* of a divine command.

Now, every mother has *power* to obtain prompt obedience,
if she commences with her children when they are young.
They are then entirely in her hands. All their enjoyments are
at her disposal. God has thus given her all the power she
needs to govern and guide them as she pleases. We have
endeavored to show . . . that the fundamental principle of
government is, *when you do give a command, invariably
enforce its obedience.* And God has given every mother the
power. He has placed in your hands a helpless babe, entirely
dependent upon you; so that if it disobeys you, all you have
to do is to cut off its sources of enjoyment, or inflict bodily
pain, so steadily and so invariably that disobedience and
suffering shall be indissolubly connected in the mind of the
child. What more *power* can a parent ask for than God has
already given? And if we fail to use this power for the purposes for which it was bestowed, the sin is ours, and upon us
and upon our children must rest the consequences. The exercise of discipline must often be painful, but if you shrink
from duty here, you expose yourself to all that sad train of
woes which disobedient children leave behind them. If you
cannot summon sufficient resolution to deprive of enjoyment
and inflict pain when it is necessary, then you must feel that a
broken heart and an old age of sorrow will not be unmerited.
And when you look upon your dissolute sons and ungrateful
daughters, you must remember that the time was when you
might have checked their evil propensities. If you love momentary ease better than your children's welfare and your
own permanent happiness, you cannot murmur at the lot you
have freely chosen. And when you meet your children at the
bar of God, and they point to you and say, "It was through
your neglect of duty that we are banished from heaven, and
consigned to endless woe," you must feel what no tongue
can tell. Ah! it is dreadful for a mother to trifle with duty.
Eternal destinies are committed to your trust. The influence

you are now exerting will go on, unchecked by the grave or the judgment, and will extend onward through those ages to which there is no end.

CHAPTER III.   MATERNAL AUTHORITY—CONTINUED

UPON the subject of obedience there are a few other suggestions of importance to be made.

1. *First then, there is a very great diversity in the natural dispositions of children.* Some are very tender in their feelings, and easily governed by affection. Others are naturally independent and self-willed. Sometimes a child gets its passions excited and its will determined, and it cannot be subdued but by a very great effort. Almost every faithful mother is acquainted with such contests, and she knows that they often form a *crisis* in the character of the child. If the child then obtain the victory, it is almost impossible for the mother afterward to regain her authority. The child feels that he is the victor, and his mother the vanquished; and it is with very great difficulty that he will be compelled to renounce his independence. If, on the other hand, the mother conquer, and the child is subdued, he feels that the question is settled, and he has but little disposition to resume hostilities with one who has proved herself superior. I have known many such contests, severe and protracted, which were exceedingly painful to a parent's feelings. But, when once entered upon, they must be continued till the child is subdued. It is not safe, on *any account,* for the parent to give up and retire vanquished.

• • • • •

It is always best, if possible, to avoid such collisions. Many children are taught implicit obedience, without ever entering into such a contest with their parents. And it is certainly preferable to govern a child by the mild procedure of ordinary discipline, rather than enter into such a formidable conflict, where great severity is often required. Wisdom, therefore, teaches us to guard against giving a child an opportunity of summoning all its energies to disobey. They are peculiar occasions, and peculiar moods of mind, which generally elicit this strength of rebellious feeling. A little foresight will often enable us, without surrender of authority, to calm the rising feeling, instead of exciting it to its utmost strength. We may sometimes, by judicious management, check the rebellion in its first appearance, before it has gained sufficient strength to call all our power into exercise to put it down.

· · · · ·

It is clear that there is a striking difference in the natural dispositions of children; but nothing can be more evident than that a good disposition may be soured by mismanagement, and that a child of naturally unamiable feelings may, by judicious culture, become mild and lovely. The cultivation of the disposition is an important part of education. Hence the necessity of studying the moods and the feelings of the child, and of varying the discipline to meet these changes. Cases will undoubtedly arise, when the parent will find it difficult to judge what is duty. Such cases will, however, be unfrequent. The obvious general policy is, when a child is in this excited state, to remove him as much as possible from the power of temptation. And if he commits a fault which it is necessary to notice, let the punishment be of such a kind as is calculated to soothe him. For instance, give him a comfortable seat by the fire, and tell him that he must not leave the chair for half an hour. Place in his hand some pleasing book, or some plaything which will amuse him. In this way let the punishment be adapted to the peculiarity of the moral disorder.

· · · · ·

3. *Never think that your child is too young to obey.* We are ingenious in framing excuses for neglecting our duty with our children. At one time they are too young; again they are too sick. Some parents always find an excuse, of one kind or another, for letting their children have their own way. A child may, at a very early age, be taught obedience. We can easily

teach a kitten, or a little dog, that it must not touch the meat which is placed before the fire, that it must leave the room when bidden, and a thousand other acts of ready obedience.

A Frenchman has recently collected a large number of canary birds for a show. He has taught them such implicit obedience to his voice, as to march them in platoons across the room, and directs them to the ready performance of many simple manœuvers.

Now, can it be admitted that a child, fifteen months or two years of age, is inferior in understanding to a canary bird? And must the excuse be made for such a child, that he does not know enough to be taught obedience? A very judicious mother, who has brought up a large family of children, all of whom are now in situations of respectability and usefulness, remarked that it was her practice to obey her children for the first year of their life, but ever after she expected them to obey her. She, of course, did not mean by this remark, that the moment the child was one year of age, a sudden and total change took place in her management. During the early months of its infancy she considered it to be her duty to do every thing in her power to make the child comfortable and happy. She would endeavor to anticipate all its wants. She would be obedient to the wishes of the child. But, by the time the child was one year of age, she considered it old enough to be brought under the salutary regulations of a well disciplined family.

I am aware that many parents will say that this is altogether too early a period to commence the government of a child, and others equally numerous, perhaps, will say that it is too late; that a beginning should be made at a much earlier period. In fact, the principle which really ought to guide in such a case, is this: that the authority of the mother ought to be established over the child as soon as it is able to understand a command or prohibition expressed by looks and gestures. This is at a much earlier period than most parents imagine. Let the mother who doubts it try the experiment, and see how easily she can teach her child that he must not touch the tongs or andirons; or that, when sitting in her lap at table, he must not touch the cups and saucers. A child may be taught obedience in such things then, as well as at any period of its life. And how much trouble does a mother save herself, by having her child thus early taught to obey! How much pain and sorrow does she save her child by accustoming it, in its most tender years, to habits of prompt obedience.

4. *Guard against too much severity.* By pursuing a steady course of efficient government, severity will very seldom be found necessary. If, when punishment is inflicted, it is done with composure and with solemnity, occasions for punishment will be very unfrequent. Let a mother ever be affectionate and mild with her children. Let her sympathise with them in their little sports. Let her gain their confidence by her assiduous efforts to make them happy. And let her feel, when they have done wrong, not irritated, but sad; and punish them in sorrow, but not in anger. Fear is a useful and a necessary principle in family government. God makes use of it in governing his creatures. But it is ruinous to the disposition of a child, exclusively to control him by this motive. How unhappy must be that family where the parent always sits with a face deformed with scowls, and where the voice is always uttered in tones of severity and command! Such parents we do see. Their children fear them. They are always under restraint in their presence; and home becomes to them an irksome prison, instead of the happy retreat of peace and joy. But where the mother greets her children with smiles; and rewards their efforts to please her, with caresses; and addresses them in tones of mildness and affection, she is touching those chords in the human heart which vibrate in sweet harmony; she is calling into action the noblest and the loveliest principles of our nature. And thus does she prepare the way for every painful act of discipline to come with effectual power upon the heart. The children know that she does not love to punish. In all cases in which it can be done, children should thus be governed by kindness. But when

kindness fails, and disobedience ensues, let not the mother hesitate for a moment to fall back upon her last resort, and punish as severely as is necessary. A few such cases will teach almost any child how much better it is to be obedient than disobedient.

By being thus consistent and decided in government, and commencing with the infancy of each child, in all ordinary cases great severity may be avoided. And it is never proper for a parent to be harsh, and unfeeling, and forbidding, in her intercourse with her children. The most efficient family government may be almost entirely administered by affection, if it be distinctly understood that disobedience cannot pass unpunished. I cannot but pity those unhappy children who dare not come to their parents in confidence and love; who are continually fearing stern looks and harsh words; and who are consequently ever desirous to get away from home, that they may enjoy themselves. Every effort should be made to make home the most desirable place; to gather around it associations of delight; and thus to form in the mind of your child an attachment for peaceful and purifying enjoyments. This will most strongly fortify his mind against vice. And when he leaves the paternal roof, he will ever look back with fond recollections to its joys, and with gratitude to those who made it the abode of so much happiness. In future years, too, when your children become the heads of families, they will transmit to their children the principles which you have implanted. Thus may the influence of your instructions extend to thousands yet unborn.

How little do we think of the tremendous responsibilities which are resting upon us; and of the wide influence, either for good or evil, which we are exerting! We are setting in operation a train of causes which will go down through all coming time. Long after we have gone to our eternal home, our words and our actions will be aiding in the formation of character. We cannot then arrest the causes which our lives have set in progress, and they will go on elevating immortals to virtue and to heaven, or urging them onward in passion, and sin, and woe.

• • • • •

CHAPTER VI.   RELIGIOUS INSTRUCTION

• • • • •

Death is succeeded by judgment, and judgment by eternity. If you are the destroyer of your child, through eternity you must bear its reproaches. You must gaze upon the wreck of its immortal spirit, while conscience says that, if you had been faithful, yourself and your child might have been reposing in heaven. Think not that you can go in one path, and induce your child to walk in another. You must not only "point to heaven," but "lead the way." The first thing to be done, is for a mother to give her own heart to God. Become a Christian yourself, and then you may hope for God's blessing upon your efforts to lead your child to the Savior. We do entreat every mother who reads these pages, as she values her own happiness and the happiness of her children, immediately to surrender her heart to God. Atoning blood has removed every difficulty from the way. The Holy Spirit is ready, in answer to your prayers, to grant you all needful assistance. Every hour that you neglect this duty, you are leading your children farther from God, and rendering the prospect of their return more hopeless.

3. *Present religion in a cheerful aspect.* There is no real enjoyment without piety. The tendency of religion is to make us happy here and hereafter; to divest the mind of gloom, and fill it with joy. Many parents err in this respect. They dwell too much upon the terrors of the law. They speak with countenances saddened and gloomy. Religion becomes to the child an unwelcome topic, and is regarded as destructive of happiness. The idea of God is associated with gloom and terror. Many parents have, in their latter years, become convinced of the injudicious course they have pursued in this respect. They

have so connected religious considerations with melancholy countenances and mournful tones of voice, as to cause the subject to be unnecessarily repugnant.

We may, indeed, err upon the other extreme. The nature of sin, and the justice of God, and the awful penalty of his law, should be distinctly exhibited. The child should be taught to regard God as that being who, while he loves his creatures, cannot look upon sin but with abhorrence. If we speak to children simply of the Creator's goodness, as manifested in the favors we are daily receiving, an erroneous impression of God's character will be conveyed. It is to be feared that many deceive themselves in thinking they love God. They have in their minds a poetic idea of an amiable and sentimental being, whose character is composed of fondness and indulgence. Such persons are as far from worshipping the true God, as is the Indian devotee or the sensual Moslem. God must be represented as he has exhibited himself to us in the Bible and in the works of nature. He is a God of mercy and of justice. He is a God of love, and a consuming fire. He is to be regarded with our warmest affections, and also with reverence and godly fear. Let, therefore, children distinctly understand that sin cannot pass unpunished. But it should also be understood that judgment is God's strange work. Ordinarily speak of his goodness. Show his readiness to forgive. Excite the gratitude of the child by speaking of the joys of heaven. Thus let the duties of religion ever be connected with feelings of enjoyment and images of happiness, that the child may perceive that gloom and sorrow are connected only with disobedience and irreligion. There is enough in the promised joys of heaven to rouse a child's most animated feelings. This subject has more to cheer the youthful heart than any other which can be presented. Appeal to gratitude. Excite hope. Speak of the promised reward. Thus may you most reasonably hope to lead your child to love its Maker, and to live for heaven. Reserve the terrors of the law for solemn occasions, when you may produce a deep and abiding impression. If you are continually introducing these motives, the mind becomes hardened against their influence; religion becomes a disagreeable topic, and the inveteracy of sin is confirmed.

• • • • •

CHAPTER VII.   RELIGIOUS INSTRUCTION — CONTINUED

• • • • •

5. *Expect that your child will become a Christian.* That the heart which is susceptible of sorrow and of love, is capable of evangelical repentance and love to God. No one can doubt but that, at a very early period in life, a child has all the powers which are employed in the exercise of true religion. Neither can there be any doubt that at that early period the mind is more susceptible of impression, the hold of the world is more feeble, and the current of affection may be more easily turned to God. And facts do hold forth most abundant encouragement. How many little memoirs have recently been issued from the press, which have told the affecting tale of youthful piety! Children of five or six years of age have given the most gratifying evidence of attachment to the Savior. They have endured pain, and met death, sustained by the consolations of religion. Such facts have been too numerous and too decisive to allow unbelief to be longer excusable. And yet it is to be feared that many parents do not feel their immediate responsibility. They still cherish the impression that their children must attain maturity before they can be decidedly penitent for sin, and the friends of God. But the mother who entertains such feelings as these, is guilty of the most cruel injustice to her child. It is almost impossible that she should be vigilant and faithful in her efforts, unless she expects success. Every mother ought to engage in the duties of religious instruction, with the confident expectation that God will accompany her exertions with his blessing. She ought even to feel that, if her child does not give early evidence of piety, much of the blame rests with her. The Christian experience of the child will undoubtedly differ from

that of the man who has passed many years in sin, whose habits are firmly fixed, and whose affections have long been flowing in the channel of worldliness. With such a person the struggle of turning to holiness will often be great, and the sense of sin distressingly intense. But the period of your child's conversion may be at so early a stage of its existence as to leave no trace by which the time of the change can be remembered. The struggle will be comparatively feeble, and penitence will be manifested by the tearful eye and the sad heart, and not always by that deep agony of spirit which not unfrequently marks the change of those who have grown old in sin.

Much injury is often done by laying stress upon the *time* when one becomes a Christian. Past feelings are at best but an uncertain test of Christian character. The great object of inquiry should be as to present feelings and conduct. Is the life now in accordance with the requirements of the Gospel? Is the heart now affected with humility, and penitence, and gratitude? Is the resolution now strong to live for God? If the sun is shining warmly upon us, it is of but little consequence at what moment it arose. There are many Christians who cannot recollect the time when they became subjects of the new birth. Be not, therefore, anxious upon this point. Indeed, by directing the attention of your child to any particular time when it became a Christian, there is danger of leading the mind to rely upon the supposed experience of that moment, rather than upon continued penitence and devotion. And therefore let every mother do all in her power to awaken in the bosoms of her children emotions of sorrow for sin, and reliance upon Christ. And when she finds these feelings in the heart, and controlling the life, let her thank God and take courage. She must watch with maternal solicitude, that temptation be avoided, and that the feeble flame burn brighter and brighter. Christ has entrusted this beloved object to your guardianship. Why should not a mother confidently expect this result to follow her efforts? Has not God encouraged her thus to hope, by promising to aid with his blessing? Has he not encouraged, by again and again crowning such efforts with success? Away then with disbelief. To doubt is to distrust the promise of God. Instruct your child, and pray for your child, and look for an immediate blessing. Thus, in all probability, will your heart be made glad by the fruits of early piety at your fire-side; grateful children will honor you through life, and the joys of heaven will be magnified by meeting your loved ones there.

• • • • •

CHAPTER VIII.   RESULTS

• • • • •

  2. *Mothers have as powerful an influence over the welfare of future generations, as all other earthly causes combined.* Thus far the history of the world has been composed of the narrations of oppression and blood. War has scattered its unnumbered woes. The cry of the oppressed has unceasingly ascended to heaven. Where are we to look for the influence which shall change this scene, and fill the earth with the fruits of peace and benevolence? It is to the power of divine truth, to Christianity, as taught from a mother's lips. In a vast majority of cases the first six or seven years decide the character of the man. If the boy leave the paternal roof uncontrolled, turbulent and vicious, he will, in all probability, rush on in the mad career of self-indulgence. There are exceptions; but these exceptions are rare. If, on the other hand, your son goes from home accustomed to control himself, he will probably retain that habit through life. If he has been taught to make sacrifices of his own enjoyment that he may promote the happiness of those around him, it may be expected that he will continue to practise benevolence, and consequently will be respected, and useful, and happy. If he has adopted firm resolutions to be faithful in all the relations in life, he, in all probability, will be a virtuous man and an estimable citizen, and a benefactor of his race.

When our land is filled with pious and patriotic mothers, then will it be filled with virtuous and patriotic men. The world's redeeming influence, under the blessing of the Holy Spirit, must come from a mother's lips. She who was first in the transgression, must be yet the principal earthly instrument in the restoration. Other causes may greatly aid. Other influences must be ready to receive the mind as it comes from the mother's hand, and carry it onward in its improvement. But the mothers of our race must be the chief instruments in its redemption. This sentiment will bear examining; and the more it is examined, the more manifestly true will it appear. It is alike the dictate of philosophy and experience. The mother who is neglecting personal effort, and relying upon other influences for the formation of virtuous character in her children, will find, when it is too late, that she has fatally erred. The patriot, who hopes that schools, and lyceums, and the general diffusion of knowledge, will promote the good order and happiness of the community, while family government is neglected, will find that he is attempting to purify the streams which are flowing from a corrupt fountain. It is maternal influence, after all, which must be the great agent, in the hands of God, in bringing back our guilty race to duty and happiness. O that mothers could feel this responsibility as they ought! Then would the world assume a different aspect. Then should we less frequently behold unhappy families and broken-hearted parents. A new race of men would enter upon the busy scene of life, and cruelty and crime would pass away. O mothers! reflect upon the power your Maker has placed in your hands! There is no earthly influence to be compared with yours. There is no combination of causes so powerful in promoting the happiness or the misery of our race, as the instructions of home. In a most peculiar sense God has constituted you the guardians and the controllers of the human family.

II.
TRANSFORMATION

10. Horace Bushnell: *Christian Nurture* (1847–61)

From at least the early 17th century through the first half of the 19th century, a succession of Christian writers argued or assumed that particular kinds of upbringing in childhood were essential for particular kinds of Christian behavior and experience in adulthood. The dominant tradition represented by the selections in this volume was the Puritan-Evangelical mode of Christianity, both in England and in America.

It was this tradition which Horace Bushnell (1802–1876) sought to change by transforming earlier methods of child rearing and altering the basic assumptions underlying attitudes toward infancy and childhood. Bushnell attacked the traditional evangelical insistence upon breaking the child's will and upon conversion experiences for membership in their churches, arguing instead that children should be reared so that they would grow into adult Christian life without having to undergo a conversion experience.

Bushnell was born in Litchfield, Connecticut, the son of a Methodist father and an Episcopalian mother, both of whom were members of the Congregationalist church at New Preston. He graduated from Yale College in 1827, studied divinity at Yale under Nathaniel W. Taylor, and in 1833 became minister of a Congregational church in Hartford, Connecticut, a position he maintained until 1859. His liberal theological views had a profound impact upon the Civil War generation.

PART ONE.   THE DOCTRINE

I. What Christian Nurture Is

"Bring them up in the nurture and admonition of the Lord."
— *Ephesians*, vi. 4.

THERE is then some kind of nurture which is of the Lord, deriving a quality and a power from Him, and communicating the same. Being instituted by Him, it will of necessity have a method and a character peculiar to itself, or rather to Him. It will be the Lord's way of education, having aims appropriate to Him, and, if realized in its full intent, terminating in results impossible to be reached by any merely human method.

What then is the true idea of Christian or divine nurture, as distinguished from that which is not Christian? What is its aim? What its method of working? What its powers and instruments? What its contemplated results? Few questions have greater moment; and it is one of the pleasant signs of the times, that the subject involved is beginning to attract new interest, and excite a spirit of inquiry which heretofore has not prevailed in our churches.

In ordinary cases, the better and more instructive way of handling this subject, would be to go directly into the practical methods of parental discipline, and show by what modes of government and instruction we may hope to realize the best results. But unhappily the public mind is preoccupied extensively by a view of the whole subject, which I must regard as a theoretical mistake, and one which will involve, as long as it continues, practical results systematically injurious. This mistaken view it is necessary, if possible, to remove. And accordingly what I have to say will take the form of an argument on the question thus put in issue; though I design to

---

Horace Bushnell, *Christian Nurture* (New York: Charles Scribner & Co., 1867), pp. 9–10, 15–18, 21–32, 56–57, 59–63, 66–68, 92–95, 101–104, 232–252, 315–320, 326–329. The original edition was published in 1847 and revised in 1861.

gather round the subject, as I proceed, as much of practical instruction as the mode of the argument will suffer. Assuming then the question above stated, What is the true idea of Christian education? — I answer in the following proposition, which it will be the aim of my argument to establish, viz:

That the child is to grow up a Christian, and never know himself as being otherwise.

In other words, the aim, effort, and expectation should be, not, as is commonly assumed, that the child is to grow up in sin, to be converted after he comes to a mature age; but that he is to open on the world as one that is spiritually renewed, not remembering the time when he went through a technical experience, but seeming rather to have loved what is good from his earliest years.

· · · · ·

There is then, as the subject appears to us —

1. No absurdity in supposing that children are to grow up in Christ. On the other hand, if there is no absurdity, there is a very clear moral incongruity in setting up a contrary supposition, to be the aim of a system of Christian education. There could not be a worse or more baleful implication given to a child, than that he is to reject God and all holy principle, till he has come to a mature age. What authority have you from the Scriptures to tell your child, or, by any sign, to show him that you do not expect him truly to love and obey God, till after he has spent whole years in hatred and wrong? What authority to make him feel that he is the most unprivileged of all human beings, capable of sin, but incapable of repentance; old enough to resist all good, but too young to receive any good whatever? It is reasonable to suppose that you have some express authority for a lesson so manifestly cruel and hurtful, else you would shudder to give it. I ask you for the chapter and verse, out of which it is derived. Meantime, wherein would it be less incongruous for you to teach your child that he is to lie and steal, and go the whole round of the

vices, and then, after he comes to mature age, reform his
conduct by the rules of virtue? Perhaps you do not give your
child to expect that he is to grow up in sin; you only expect
that he will yourself. That is scarcely better: for that which is
your expectation, will assuredly be his; and what is more, any
attempt to maintain a discipline at war with your own secret
expectations, will only make a hollow and worthless figment
of that which could be an open, earnest reality. You will
never practically aim at what you practically despair of, and if
you do not practically aim to unite your child to God, you
will aim at some thing less; that is, something unchristian,
wrong, sinful.

But my child is a sinner, you will say; and how can I
expect him to begin a right life, until God gives him a new
heart? This is the common way of speaking, and I state the
objection in its own phraseology, that it may recognize itself.
Who then has told you that a child can not have the new heart
of which you speak? Whence do you learn that if you live the
life of Christ, before him and with him, the law of the Spirit of
Life may not be such as to include and quicken him also?
And why should it be thought incredible that there should be
some really good principle awakened in the mind of a child?
For this is all that is implied in a Christian state. The Christian is one who has simply *begun* to love what is good for its
own sake, and why should it be thought impossible for a child
to have this love begotten in him? Take any scheme of depravity you please, there is yet nothing in it to forbid the
possibility that a child should be led, in his first moral act, to
cleave unto what is good and right, any more than in the first
of his twentieth year. He is, in that case, only a child converted to good, leading a mixed life as all Christians do. The
good in him goes into combat with the evil, and holds a
qualified sovereignty. And why may not this internal conflict
of goodness cover the whole life from its dawn, as well as any
part of it? And what more appropriate to the doctrine of
spiritual influence itself, than to believe that as the Spirit of

Jehovah fills all the worlds of matter, and holds a presence of power and government in all objects, so all human souls, the infantile as well as the adult, have a nurture of the Spirit appropriate to their age and their wants? What opinion is more essentially monstrous, in fact, than that which regards the Holy Spirit as having no agency in the immature souls of children who are growing up, helpless and unconscious, into the perils of time?

2. It is to be expected that Christian education will radically differ from that which is not Christian. Now, it is the very character and mark of all unchristian education, that it brings up the child for future conversion. No effort is made, save to form a habit of outward virtue, and, if God please to convert the family to something higher and better, after they come to the age of maturity, it is well. Is then Christian education, or the nurture of the Lord, no way different from this? Or is it rather to be supposed that it will have a higher aim and a more sacred character?

And, since it is the distinction of Christian parents, that they are themselves in the nurture of the Lord, since Christ and the Divine Love, communicated through him, are become the food of their life, what, will they so naturally seek as to have their children partakers with them, heirs together with them, in the grace of life? I am well aware of the common impression that Christian education is sufficiently distinguished by the endeavor of Christian parents to teach their children the lessons of Scripture history, and the doctrines or dogmas of Scripture theology. But if they are given to understand, at the same time, that these lessons can be expected to produce no fruit till they are come to a mature age — that they are to grow up still in the same character as other children do, who have no such instruction — what is this but to enforce the practical rejection of all the lessons taught them? And which, in truth, is better for them, to grow up in sin under Scripture light, with a heart hardened by so many religious lessons; or to grow up in sin, unvexed and unan-

noyed by the wearisome drill of lectures that only discourage
all practical benefit? Which is better, to be piously brought up
in sin, or to be allowed quietly to vegetate in it?

These are questions that I know not how to decide; but the
doubt in which they leave us will at least suffice to show that
Christian education has, in this view, no such eminent advantages over that which is unchristian, as to raise any broad and
dignified distinction between them. We certainly know that
much of what is called Christian nurture, only serves to make
the subject of religion odious, and that, as nearly as we can
discover, in exact proportion to the amount of religious teaching received. And no small share of the difficulty to be over-
come afterwards, in the struggle of conversion, is created in
just this way.

· · · · ·

4. Assuming the corruption of human nature, when should
we think it wisest to undertake or expect a remedy? When
evil is young and pliant to good, or when it is confirmed by
years of sinful habit? And when, in fact, is the human heart
found to be so ductile to the motives of religion, as in the
simple, ingenuous age of childhood? How easy is it then, as
compared with the stubbornness of adult years, to make all
wrong seem odious, all good lovely and desirable. If not
discouraged by some ill-temper which bruises all the gentle
sensibilities, or repelled by some technical view of religious
character which puts it beyond his age, how ready is the child
to be taken by good, as it were beforehand, and yield his
ductile nature to the truth and Spirit of God, and to a fixed
prejudice against all that God forbids.

He can not understand, of course, in the earliest stage of
childhood, the philosophy of religion as a renovated experience, and that is not the form of the first lessons he is to
receive. He is not to be told that he must have a new heart
and exercise faith in Christ's atonement. We are to understand, that a right spirit may be virtually exercised in children, when, as yet, it is not intellectually received, or as a

form of doctrine. Thus, if they are put upon an effort to be good, connecting the fact that God desires it and will help them in the endeavor, that is all which, in a very early age, they can receive, and that includes every thing—repentance, love, duty, dependence, faith. Nay, the operative truth necessary to a new life, may possibly be communicated through and from the parent, being revealed in his looks, manners, and ways of life, before they are of an age to understand the teaching of words; for the Christian scheme, the gospel, is really wrapped up in the life of every Christian parent, and beams out from him as a living epistle, before it escapes from the lips, or is taught in words. And the Spirit of truth may as well make this living truth effectual, as the preaching of the gospel itself.

Never is it too early for good to be communicated. Infancy and childhood are the ages most pliant to good. And who can think it necessary that the plastic nature of childhood must first be hardened into stone, and stiffened into enmity towards God and all duty, before it can become a candidate for Christian character! There could not be a more unnecessary mistake, and it is as unnatural and pernicious, I fear, as it is unnecessary.

There are many who assume the radical goodness of human nature, and the work of Christian education is, in their view, only to educate or educe the good that is in us. Let no one be disturbed by the suspicion of a coincidence between what I have here said and such a theory. The natural pravity of man is plainly asserted in the Scriptures, and, if it were not, the familiar laws of physiology would require us to believe, what amounts to the same thing. And if neither Scripture nor physiology taught us the doctrine, if the child was born as clear of natural prejudice or damage, as Adam before his sin, spiritual education, or, what is the same, probation, that which trains a being for a stable, intelligent virtue hereafter, would still involve an experiment of evil, therefore a fall and a bondage under the laws of evil; so that, view the matter as we will, there is no so unreasonable assumption, none so wide of all just philosophy, as that which proposes to form a child to virtue, by simply educing or drawing out what is in him.

The growth of Christian virtue is no vegetable process, no mere onward development. It involves a struggle with evil, a fall and a rescue. The soul becomes established in holy virtue, as a free exercise, only as it is passed round the corner of fall and redemption, ascending thus unto God through a double experience, in which it learns the bitterness of evil and the worth of good, fighting its way out of one, and achieving the other as a victory. The child, therefore, may as well begin life under a law of hereditary damage, as to plunge himself into evil by his own experiment, which he will as naturally do from the simple impulse of curiosity, or the instinct of knowledge, as from any noxious quality in his mold derived by descent. For it is not sin which he derives from his parents; at least, not sin in any sense which imports blame, but only some prejudice to the perfect harmony of this mold, some kind of pravity or obliquity which inclines him to evil. These suggestions are offered, not as necessary to be received in every particular, but simply to show that the scheme of education proposed, is not to be identified with another, which assumes the radical goodness of human nature, and according to which, if it be true, Christian education is insignificant.

5. It is implied in all our religious philosophy, that if a child ever does any thing in a right spirit, ever loves any thing because it is good and right, it involves the dawn of a new life. This we can not deny or doubt, without bringing in question our whole scheme of doctrine. Is it then incredible that some really good feeling should be called into exercise in a child? In all the discipline of the house, quickened as it should be by the Spirit of God, is it true that he can never once be brought to submit to parental authority lovingly and because it is right? Must we even hold the absurdity of the scripture council—"Children obey your parents in the Lord, for this is right?" When we speak thus of a love for what is right and good, we must of course discriminate between the mere excitement of a natural sensibility to pleasure in the

contemplation of what is good (of which the worst minds are more or less capable,) and a practicable subordination of the soul to its power, a practicable embrace of its law. The child must not only be touched with some gentle emotions toward what is right, but he must love it with a fixed love, love it for the sake of its principle, receive it as a vital and formative power.

Nor is there any age, which offers itself to God's truth and love, and to that Quickening Spirit whence all good proceeds, with so much of ductile feeling and susceptibilities so tender. The child is under parental authority too for the very purpose, it would seem, of having the otherwise abstract principle of all duty impersonated in his parents, and thus brought home to his practical embrace; so that, learning to obey his parents in the Lord, because it is right, he may thus receive, before he can receive it intellectually, the principle of all piety and holy obedience. And when he is brought to exercise a spirit of true and loving submission to the good law of his parents, what will you see, many times, but a look of childish joy, and a happy sweetness of manner, and a ready delight in authority, as like to all the demonstrations of Christian experience, as any thing childish can be to what is mature?

6. Children have been so trained as never to remember the time when they began to be religious. Baxter was, at one time, greatly troubled concerning himself, because he could recollect no time when there was a gracious change in his character. But he discovered, at length, that "education is as properly a means of grace as preaching," and thus found the sweeter comfort in his love to God, that he learned to love him so early. The European churches, generally, regard Christian piety more as a habit of life, formed under the training of childhood, and less as a marked spiritual change in experience. In Germany, for example, the church includes all the people, and it is remarkable that, under a scheme so loose, and with so much of pernicious error taught in the pulpit, there is yet so much of deep religious feeling, so much of lovely and simple character, and a savor of Christian piety

so generally prevalent in the community. So true is this, that the German people are every day spoken of as a people religious by nature; no other way being observed of accounting for the strong religious bent they manifest. Whereas it is due, beyond any reasonable question, to the fact that children are placed under a form of treatment which expects them to be religious, and are not discouraged by the demand of an experience above their years.

Again, the Moravian Brethren, it is agreed by all, give as ripe and graceful an exhibition of piety, as any body of Christians living on the earth, and it is the radical distinction of their system that it rests its power on Christian education. They make their churches schools of holy nurture to childhood, and expect their children to grow up there, as plants in the house of the Lord. Accordingly it is affirmed that not one in ten of the members of that church, recollects any time when he began to be religious. Is it then incredible that what has been can be? Would it not be wiser and more modest, when facts are against us, to admit that there is certainly some bad error, either in our life, or in our doctrine, or in both, which it becomes us to amend?

Once more, if we narrowly examine the relation of parent and child, we shall not fail to discover something like a law or organic connection, as regards character, subsisting between them. Such a connection as makes it easy to believe, and natural to expect, that the faith of the one will be propagated in the other. Perhaps I should rather say, such a connection as induces the conviction that the character of one is actually included in that of the other, as a seed is formed in the capsule; and being there matured, by a nutriment derived from the stem, is gradually separated from it. It is a singular fact, that many believe substantially the same thing, in regard to evil character, but have no thought of any such possibility in regard to good. There has been much speculation, of late, as to whether a child is born in depravity, or whether the depraved character is superinduced afterwards. But, like many other great questions, it determines much less than is commonly supposed; for, according to the most proper view of the subject, a child is really not born till he emerges from the infantile state, and never before that time can he be said to receive a separate and properly individual nature.

The declarations of Scripture, and the laws of physiology, I have already intimated, compel the belief that a child's nature is somehow depravated by descent from parents, who are under the corrupting effects of sin. But this, taken as a question relating to the mere *punctum temporis,* or precise point of birth, is not a question of any so grave import as is generally supposed; for the child, after birth, is still within the matrix of the parental life, and will be, more or less, for many years. And the parental life will be flowing into him all that time, just as naturally, and by a law as truly organic, as when the sap of the trunk flows into a limb. We must not govern our thoughts, in such a matter, by our eyes; and because the physical separation has taken place, conclude that no organic relation remains. Even the physical being of the child is dependent still for many months, in the matter of nutrition, on organic processes not in itself. Meantime, the mental being and character have scarcely begun to have a proper individual life. Will in connection with conscience, is the basis of personality, or individuality, and these exist as yet only in their rudimental type, as when the form of a seed is beginning to be unfolded at the root of a flower.

At first, the child is held as a mere passive lump in the arms, and he opens into conscious life under the soul of the parent, streaming into his eyes and ears, through the manners and tones of the nursery. The kind and degree of passivity are gradually changed as life advances. A little farther on it is observed that a smile wakens a smile; any kind of sentiment or passion, playing in the face of the parent, wakens a responsive sentiment or passion. Irritation irritates, a frown withers, love expands a look congenial to itself, and why not holy love? Next the ear is opened to the understanding of words, but what words the child shall hear, he can not choose, and has as little capacity to select the sentiments that are poured into his soul. Farther on, the parents begin to govern him by appeals to will, expressed in commands, and whatever their requirement may be, he can as little withstand it, as the violet can cool the scorching sun, or the tattered leaf can tame the hurricane. Next they appoint his school, choose his books, regulate his company, decide what form of religion, and what religious opinions he shall be taught, by taking him to a church of their own selection. In all this, they infringe upon no right of the child, they only fulfill an office which belongs to them. Their will and character are designed to be the matrix of the child's will and character. Meantime, he approaches more and more closely, and by a gradual process, to the proper rank and responsibility of an individual creature, during all which process of separation, he is having their exercises and ways translated into him. Then, at last, he comes forth to act his part in such color of evil, and why not of good, as he has derived from them.

The tendency of all our modern speculations is to an extreme individualism, and we carry our doctrines of free will so far as to make little or nothing of organic laws; not observing that character may be, to a great extent, only the free development of exercises previously wrought in us, or extended to us, when other wills had us within their sphere. All the Baptist theories of religion are based in this error. They assume, as a first truth, that no such thing is possible as an organic connection of character, an assumption which is plainly refuted by what we see with our eyes, and, as I shall by and by show, by the declarations of Scripture. We have much to say also, in common with the Baptists, about the beginning of moral agency, and we seem to fancy that there is some definite moment when a child becomes a moral agent, passing out of a condition where he is a moral nullity, and where no moral agency touches his being. Whereas he is rather to be regarded, at the first, as lying within the moral agency of the parent, and passing out, by degrees, through a course of mixed agency, to a proper independency and self-possession. The supposition that he becomes, at some certain moment, a complete moral agent, which a moment before he was not, is clumsy, and has no agreement with observation. The separation is gradual. He is never, at any moment after birth, to be regarded as perfectly beyond the sphere of good and bad exercises; for the parent exercises himself in the child, playing his emotions and sentiments, and working a character in him, by virtue of an organic power.

And this is the very idea of Christian education, that it begins with nurture or cultivation. And the intention is that the Christian life and spirit of the parents, which are in and by the Spirit of God, shall flow into the mind of the child, to blend with his incipient and half-formed exercises; that they shall thus beget their own good within him — their thoughts, opinions, faith, and love, which are to become a little more, and yet a little more, his own separate exercise, but still the same in character. The contrary assumption, that virtue must be the product of separate and absolutely independent choice, is pure assumption. As regards the measure of personal merit and demerit, it is doubtless true that every subject of God is to be responsible only for what is his own. But virtue still is rather a *state* of being than an act or series of acts; and, if we look at the causes which induce or prepare such a state, the will of the person himself may have a part among these causes more or less important, and it works no absurdity to suppose that one may be even prepared to such a state, by causes prior to his own will; so that, when he sets off to act for himself, his struggle and duty may be rather to sustain and perfect the state begun, than to produce a new one. Certain it is that we are never, at any age, so independent as to be wholly out of the reach of organic laws which affect our character.

All society is organic — the church, the state, the school, the family; and there is a spirit in each of these organisms, peculiar to itself, and more or less hostile, more or less favorable to religious character, and to some extent, at least, sovereign over the individual man. A very great share of the power in what is called a revival of religion, is organic power;

nor is it any the less divine on that account. The child is only more within the power of organic laws than we all are. We possess only a mixed individuality all our life long. A pure, separate, individual man, living *wholly* within, and from himself, is a mere fiction. No such person ever existed, or ever can. I need not say that this view of an organic connection of character subsisting between parent and child, lays a basis for notions of Christian education, far different from those which now prevail, under the cover of a merely fictitious and mischievous individualism.

Perhaps it may be necessary to add, that, in the strong language I have used concerning the organic connection of character between the parent and the child, it is not designed to assert a power in the parent to renew the child, or that the child can be renewed by any agency of the Spirit less immediate, than that which renews the parent himself. When a germ is formed on the stem of any plant, the formative instinct of the plant may be said in one view to produce it; but the same solar heat which quickens the plant, must quicken also the germ, and sustain the internal action of growth, by a common presence in both. So, if there be an organic power of character in the parent, such as that of which I have spoken, it is not a complete power in itself, but only such a power as demands the realizing presence of the Spirit of God, both in the parent and the child, to give it effect. As Paul said, "I have begotten you through the gospel," so may we say of the parent, who, having a living gospel enveloped in his life, brings it into organic connection with the soul of childhood. But the declaration excludes the necessity of a divine influence, not more in one case than in the other.

Such are some of the considerations that offer themselves, viewing our subject on the human side, or as it appears in the light of human evidence—all concurring to produce the conviction, that it is the only true idea of Christian education, that the child is to grow up in the life of the parent, and be a Christian in principle, from his earliest years.

II.   WHAT CHRISTIAN NURTURE IS

• • • • •

What motives are laid upon all Christian parents, by the doctrine I have established, to make the first article of family discipline a constant and careful discipline of themselves. I would not undervalue a strong and decided government in families. No family can be rightly trained without it. But there is a kind of virtue, my brethren, which is not in the rod — the virtue, I mean, of a truly good and sanctified life. And a reign of brute force is much more easily maintained, than a reign whose power is righteousness and love. There are, too, I must warn you, many who talk much of the rod as the orthodox symbol of parental duty, but who might really as well be heathens as Christians; who only storm about their house with heathenish ferocity, who lecture, and threaten, and castigate, and bruise, and call this family government. They even dare to speak of this as the nurture of the Lord. So much easier is it to be violent than to be holy, that they substitute force for goodness and grace, and are wholly un-conscious of the imposture. It is frightful to think how they batter and bruise the delicate, tender souls of their children, extinguishing in them what they ought to cultivate, crushing that sensibility which is the hope of their being, and all in the sacred name of Christ Jesus. By no such summary process can you dispatch your duties to your children. You are not to be a savage to them, but a father and a Christian. Your real aim and study must be to infuse into them a new life, and, to this end, the Life of God must perpetually reign in you. Gathered round you as a family, they are all to be so many motives, strong as the love you bear them, to make you Christ-like in your spirit. It must be seen and felt with them that religion is a first thing with you. And it must be first, not in words and talk, but visibly first in your love — that which fixes your aims, feeds your enjoyments, sanctifies your plea-sures, supports your trials, satisfies your wants, contents your ambition, beautifies and blesses your character. No mock piety, no sanctimony of phrase, or longitude of face on Sundays will suffice. You must live in the light of God, and hold such a spirit in exercise as you wish to see translated into your children. You must take them into your feeling as a loving and joyous element, and beget, if by the grace of God you may, the spirit of your own heart in theirs.

• • • • •

It is to be deeply considered, in connection with this view of family nurture, whether it does not meet many of the deficiencies we deplore in the Christian character of our times, and the present state of our churches. We have been expecting to thrive too much by conquest, and too little by growth. I desire to speak with all caution of what are very unfortunately called revivals of religion; for apart from the name, which is modern, and from certain crudities and excesses that go with it — which name, crudities, and excesses are wholly adventitious as regards the substantial merits of such scenes — apart from these, I say, there is abundant reason to believe that God's spiritual economy includes varieties of exercise, answering, in all important respects, to these visitations of mercy, so much coveted in our churches. They are needed. A perfectly uniform demonstration in religion is not possible or desirable. Nothing is thus uniform but death. Our exercise varies every year and day from childhood onward. Society is going through new modes of exercise in the same manner, excited by new subjects, running into new types of feeling, and struggling with new combinations of thought. Quite as necessary is it that all holy principle should have a varied exercise — now in one duty, now in another; now in public aims and efforts, now in bosom struggles; now in social methods, now in those which are solitary and private; now in high emotion, now in deliberative thought and study. Accordingly the Christian church began with a scene of extraordinary social demonstration, and the like, in one form or another, may be traced in every period of its history since that day.

But the difficulty is with us that we idolize such scenes, and make them the whole of our religion. We assume that nothing good is doing, or can be done at any other time. And what is even worse, we often look upon these scenes, and desire them, rather as scenes of victory, than of piety. They are the harvest-times of conversion, and conversion is too nearly every thing with us. In particular we see no way to gather in disciples, save by means of certain marked experiences, developed in such scenes, in adult years. Our very children can possibly come to no good, save in this way. Instrumentalities are invented to compass our object, that are only mechanical, and the hope of mere present effect is supposed to justify them. Present effect, in the view of many, justifies any thing and every thing. We strain every nerve of motion, exhaust every capacity of endurance, and push on till nature sinks in exhaustion. We preach too much, and live Christ too little. We do many things which, in a cooler mood, are seen to hurt the dignity of religion, and which somewhat shame and sicken ourselves. Hence the present state of religion in our country [ca. 1846]. We have worked a vein till it has run out. The churches are exhausted. There is little to attract them, when they look upon the renewal of scenes through which many of them have passed. They look about them, with a sigh, to ask if possibly there is no better way, and some are ready to find that better way, in a change of their religion. Nothing different from this ought to have been expected. No nation can long thrive by a spirit of conquest; no more can a church. There must be an internal growth, that is made by holy industry, in the common walks of life and duty. . . .

Then also the piety of the coming age will be deeper, and more akin to habit than ours, because it began earlier. It will have more of an air of naturalness, and will be less a work of will. A generation will come forward, who will have been educated to all good undertakings and enterprises—ardent without fanaticism, powerful without machinery. Not born, so generally, in a storm, and brought to Christ by an abrupt transition, the latter portion of life will not have an unequal war to maintain with the beginning, but life will be more nearly one, and in harmony with itself. Is not this a result to be desired? Could we tell our American churches, at this moment, what they want, should we not tell them this? Neither, if God, as many fear, is about to bring upon his church a day of wrath and stormy conflict, let any one suspect that such a kind of piety will want vigor and nerve to withstand the fiery assaults anticipated. See what turn the mind of our apostle took when he was arming his disciples for the great conflict of their age. Children, obey your parents — Fathers, provoke not your children — Servants, be obedient to your masters — Masters, forbear threatening — Finally, to include all, put on the whole armor of God. As if the first thought, in arming the church for great trials and stout victories, was to fill common life and the relations of the house with a Christian spirit. There is no truer truth, or more sublime. Religion never thoroughly penetrates life, till it becomes domestic. Like that patriotic fire which makes a nation invincible, it never burns with inextinguishable devotion till it burns at the hearth.

•••••

III. THE OSTRICH NURTURE

•••••

As a curious illustration of the looseness and the unsettled feeling of the times, in regard to this great subject, it is just now beginning to be asserted by some, that the true principle of training for children is exactly that of the ostrich, viz: no training at all; the best government, no government. All endeavors to fashion them by the parental standards, or to induct them into the belief of their parents, is alleged to be a real oppression put upon their natural liberty. It is nothing less, it is said, than an effort to fill them with prejudices, and put them under the sway of prejudices, all their lives long. Why not let the child have his own way, think his own thoughts, generate his own principles, and so be developed in the freedom and beauty of the flowers? Or, if he should sometimes fall into bad tempers and disgraceful or uncomely practices, as flowers do not, let him learn how to correct *himself,* and be righted by his own discoveries. Having thus no artificial conscience formed to hamper his natural freedom, no religious scruples and superstitions inculcated to be a detention, or limitation, upon his impulses, he will grow up as a genuine character, stunted by no cant or affection; a large-minded, liberal, original, and beautiful soul.

This kind of nurture supposes, evidently, a faith in human nature that is total and complete. As the mother ostrich might be supposed to reason, that her eggs are ostrich's eggs, and must therefore produce genuine ostriches and nothing else, so it assumes that human children will grow up, left to themselves, into the most genuine, highest style of human character. Whereas, it is the misery of human children that, as free beings, answerable for their choices and their character, and already touched with evil, they require some training, over and above the mere indulgence of their natural instincts. They can not be left to merely blossom into character; or, if they are, it will most assuredly be any sort of character but that which parental love would desire. What they most especially want is, what no ostrich or mere animal nurture can give; to be preoccupied with holy principles and laws; to have prejudices instilled that are holy prejudices; and so to be tempered beforehand by moderating and guiding influences, such as their perilous freedom and hereditary damage require.

• • • • •

IV.   THE ORGANIC UNITY OF THE FAMILY

• • • • •

What then do we mean by the organic unity of the family? It will be understood, of course, that we do not speak of a physical or vascular connection; for, after birth, there is no such connection existing, any more than there is between persons of different families. In so far, however, as a connection of parentage, or derivation has affected the character, that fact must be included, though it can not be regarded as a chief element in the unity asserted. Perhaps I shall be understood with the greatest facility, if I say that the family is such a body, that a power over character is exerted therein, *which can not properly be called influence*. We commonly use the term *influence* to denote a persuasive power, or a governmental power, exerted purposely, and with a conscious design to effect some result in the subject. In maintaining the organic unity of the family, I mean to assert, that a power is exerted by parents over children, not only when they teach, encourage, persuade, and govern, but without any purposed control whatever. The bond is so intimate that they do it unconsciously and undesignedly — they must do it. Their character, feelings, spirit, and principles, must propagate themselves, whether they will or not. However, as influence, in the sense just given, can not be *received* by childhood prior to the age of reason and deliberative choice, the control of parents, purposely exerted, must be regarded, during that early period, as an absolute force, not as influence. All such acts of control therefore must, in metaphysical propriety, and as far as the child is concerned, be classed under the general denomination of *organic* causes. And thus whatever power over character is exerted in families one side of consent, in the children, and even before they have come to the age of rational choice, must be taken as organic power, in the same way as if the effect accrued under the law of simple contagion. So too when the child performs acts of will, under parental direction, that involve results of character, without knowing or considering that they do, these must be classed in the same manner.

In general, then, we find the organic unity of the family, in every exertion of power over character, which is not exerted and received as influence; that is, with a *design* to address the choice on one side, and *a sense* of responsible choice on the other. Or, to use language more popular, we conceive the manners, personal views, prejudices, practical motives, and spirit of the house, as an atmosphere which passes into all and pervades all, as naturally as the air they breathe. This, however, not in any such absolute or complete sense as to leave no room for individual distinctions. Sometimes the two parents will have a very different spirit themselves, though the grace of God is pledged to make the better, if it be truly right, and hindered by no gross inconsistencies, victorious. Sometimes the child, passing into the sphere of other causes, as in the school, the church, neighboring families, or general society, will emerge and take a character partially distinct—partially, I say; never wholly. The odor of the house will always be in his garments, and the internal difficulties with which he has to struggle, will spring of the family seeds planted in his nature.

Having carefully stated thus what I mean by the organic unity of the family, I next proceed to inquire whether any such unity exists? And here it is worth noticing—

1. That there is nothing in this view which conflicts with the proper individuality of persons and their separate responsibility. We have gained immense advantages, in modern times, as regards society, government, and character, by liberating and exalting the individual man. Far be it from me to underrate these advantages, or to bring them into jeopardy. But a child manifestly can not be a proper individual, before he is one. Nothing can be gained by assuming that he is; and, if it is not true, much is sure to be lost. Besides, we are never, at any age, so completely individual as to be clear of organic connections that affect our character. To a certain extent and

for certain purposes, we are individuals, acting each from his own will. Then to a certain extent and for certain other purposes, we are parts or members of a common body, as truly as the limbs of a tree. We have an open side in our nature, where a common feeling enters, where we adhere, and through which we are actuated by a common will. There we are many — here we are one.

• • • • •

3. We shall find that there is a law of connection, after birth, under which power over character is exerted, without any design to do it. For a considerable time after birth, the child has no capacity of will and choice developed, and therefore is not a subject of influence, in the common sense of that term. He is not as yet a complete individual; he has only powers and capacities that prepare him to be, when they are unfolded. They are in him only as wings and a capacity to fly are in the egg. Meantime, he is open to *impressions* from every thing he sees. His character is forming, under a principle, not of choice, but of nurture. The spirit of the house is breathed into his nature, day by day. The anger and gentleness, the fretfulness and patience — the appetites, passions, and manners — all the variant moods of feeling exhibited round him, pass into him as impressions, and become seeds of character in him; not because the parents will, but because it must be so, whether they will or not. They propagate their own evil in the child, not by design, but under a law of moral infection. Before the children begin to gather wood for the sacrifice, the spirit of the idol and his faith has been communicated. The airs and feelings and conduct of idolatry have filled their nature with impressions, which are back of all choice and memory. Go out to them then, as they are gathering faggots for the idol sacrifice, ask them what questions they have had about the service of the god? what doubts? whether any unsatisfied debate or perplexing struggle has visited their minds? and you will probably awaken their first

thoughts on the subject by the inquiry itself. All because they have grown up in the idol worship, from a point back of memory. They received it through their impressions, before they were able to receive it from choice. And so it is with all the moral transactions of the house. The spirit of the house is in the members by nurture, not by teaching, not by any attempt to communicate the same, but because it is the air the children breathe.

Now, it is in the twofold manner set forth, under this and the previous head of my discourse, that our race have fallen, as a race, into moral corruption and apostasy. In these two methods, the race have been subjected, as an organic unity, to evil; so that when they come to the age of proper individuality, the damage received has prepared them to set forth, on a course of blamable and guilty transgression. The question of original or imputed sin has been much debated in modern times, and the effort has been to vindicate the personal responsibility of each individual, as a moral agent. Nor is any thing more clear, on first principles, than that no man is responsible for any sin but his own. The sin of no person can be transmitted as a sin, or charged to the account of another. But it does not therefore follow, that there are no moral connections between individuals, by which one becomes a corrupter of others. If we are units, so also are we a race, and the race is one — one family, one organic whole; such that the fall of the head involves the fall of all the members. Under the old doctrines of original sin, federal headship, and the like, cast away by many, ridiculed by not a few, there yet lies a great and momentous truth, announced by reason as clearly as by Scripture — that in Adam all die; that by one man's disobedience many were made sinners; that death hath passed upon all men, for that all have sinned. Not that this original scheme of unity is any disadvantage. I firmly believe and think I could show the contrary even. Enough that so the Scriptures speak, and that so we see, by inspection itself. There can be no greater credulity, than for any man to expect that a sinful and death-struck being, one who has fallen out of the harmony of his mold by sin, should yet communicate no trace of evil from himself, no diseased or damaged quality, no moral discolor, to the generations that derive their existence from him. To make that possible, every law of physiology must be adjourned, and, what is more, all that we see with our eyes, in the eventful era of impressions, must be denied.

I am well aware that those who have advocated, in former times, the church dogma of original sin, as well as those who adhere to it now, speak only of a taint derived by natural or physical propagation, and do not include the taint derived afterwards, under the law of family infection. It certainly can be no heresy to include the latter; and, since it is manifest that both fall within the same general category of organic connection, it is equally manifest that both ought to be included, and, in all systematic reasonings, must be. If, during the age of impressions in the child, and previous to the development of will, a power is exerted over character — exerted necessarily, both as regards the sinful parent and the child, and that as truly as if it fell within the laws of propagation itself — it can not be right to attribute the moral taint wholly, or even principally, to propagation. Until the child comes to his will, we must regard him still as held within the matrix of the parental life; and then, when he is ripe for responsible choice, as born for action — a proper and complete person. Taking this comprehensive view of the organic unity of successive generations of men, the truth we assert of human depravation is not a half-truth exaggerated, (which many will not regard as any truth at all,) but it is a broad, well-authenticated doctrine, which no intelligent observer of facts and principles can deny. It shows the past descending on the present, the present on the future, by an inevitable law, and yet gives every parent the hope of mitigating the sad legacy of mischief he entails upon his children, by whatever improvements of character and conduct he is able to make — a hope which Christian promise so far clears to his view, as even to allow him the presumption that his child may be set forth into responsible action, as a Christian person.

• • • • •

PART TWO.   THE MODE

I.   When and Where the Nurture Begins

• • • • •

Here, then, is the real and true beginning of a godly nurture. The child is not to have the sad entail of any sensuality,
or excess, or distempered passion upon him. The heritage of
love, peace, order, continence and holy courage is to be his.
He is not to be morally weakened beforehand, in the womb of
folly, by the frivolous, worldly, ambitious, expectations of
parents-to-be, concentrating all their nonsense in him. His
affinities are to be raised by the godly expectations, rather,
and prayers that go before; by the steady and good aims of
their industry, by the great impulse of their faith, by the
brightness of their hope, by the sweet continence of their
religiously pure love in Christ. Born, thus, of a parentage that
is ordered in all righteousness, and maintains the right use of
every thing, especially the right use of nature and marriage,
the child will have just so much of heaven's life and order in
him beforehand, as have become fixed properties in the type
of his parentage; and by this ante-natal nurture, will be set off
in a way of noblest advantage, as respects all safety and
success, in the grand experiment he has come into the world
to make.

Having called your attention to this very important but
strangely disregarded chapter, in the economy of Christian
nurture, I leave it to be more fully circumstantially developed
by your own thoughtful consideration; for it is a matter which
will open itself readily, and prove itself by striking and continually recurring facts to such as have it in their hearts to watch
for the truth and the duties it requires. We pass now —

2. To that which is the common field of inquiry, and here
we raise again the question, where and how early does the
work of nurture begin? here to set forth and maintain still
another answer, which antedates the common impression,

about as decidedly as the one just given. The true, and only
true answer is, that the nurture of the soul and character is to
begin just when the nurture of the body begins. It is first to be
infantile nurture—as such, Christian; then to be a child's
nurture; then to be a youth's nurture—advancing by imper-
ceptible gradations, if possible, according to the gradations
and stages of the growth, or progress toward maturity.

There is, of course, no absolute classification to be made
here, because there are no absolute lines of distinction. A
kind of proximate and partly ideal distinction may be made,
and I make it simply to serve the convenience of my subject—otherwise impossible to be handled, so as to secure any
right practical conviction respecting it. It is the distinction
between the age of *impressions* and the age of *tuitional
influences;* or between the age of *existence in the will of the
parent,* and the age of *will and personal choice in the child.* If
the distinction were laid, between the age previous to language and the age of language, it would amount to nearly the
same thing; for the time of personal and responsible choice
depends on the measure of intelligence attained to, and the
measure of intelligence is well represented, outwardly, by the
degree of development in language. Of course it will be understood that we speak, in this distinction, of that which is
not sharply defined, and is passed at no precise date or age.
The transition is gradual, and it will even be doubtful, when it
is passed. No one can say just where a given child passes out
of the field of mere impression into the field of responsible
action. It will be doubtful, in about the same degree, when it
can be said to have come into the power of language. We do
not even know that there is not some infinitesimal development of will in the child's first cry, and some instinct of
language struggling in that cry. Our object in the distinction is
not to assume any thing in respect to such matters, but simply
to accommodate our own ignorance, by raising a distribution
that enables us to speak of times and characteristics truly
enough to serve the conditions of general accuracy, and to
assist, in that manner, the purposes of our discussion.

Now the very common assumption is that, in what we have called the age of impressions, there is really nothing done, or to be done, for the religious character. The lack of all genuine apprehensions, in respect to this matter, among people otherwise intelligent and awake, is really wonderful; it amounts even to a kind of coarseness. Full of all fondness, and all highest expectation respecting their children, and having also many Christian desires for their welfare, they seem never to have brought their minds down close enough to the soul of infancy, to imagine that any thing of consequence is going on with it. What can they do, till they can speak to it? what can it do, till it speaks? As if there were no process going on to bring it forward into language; or as if that process had itself nothing to do with the bringing on of intelligence, and no deep, seminal working toward a character, unfolding and to be unfolded in it. The child, in other words, is to come into intelligence through perfect unintelligence! to get the power of words out of words themselves, and without any experience whereby their meaning is developed! to be taught responsibility under moral and religious ideas, when the experience has unfolded no such ideas! In this first stage, therefore, which I have called the stage of impressions, how very commonly will it be found that the parents, even Christian parents, discharge themselves, in the most innocently unthinking way possible, of so much as a conception of responsibility. The child can not talk, what then can it know? So they dress it in all fineries, practice it in shows and swells and all the petty airs of foppery and brave assumption, act it into looks and manners not fit to be acted any where, provoking the repetition of its bad tricks by laughing at them, indulging freely every sort of temper towards it, or, if may be, filling the house with a din of scolding between the parents — all this in simple security, as if their child were only a thing, or an ape! What hurt can the simple creature get from any thing done before it, toward it, or upon it, when it can talk of nothing, and will not so much as remember any thing it has seen or heard? Doubtless there is a wise care to be had of it, when it is old enough to be taught and commanded, but till then there is nothing to be done, but simply to foster the plaything kindly, enjoy it freely, or abuse it pettishly, at pleasure!

Just contrary to this, I suspect, and I think it can also be shown by sufficient evidence, that more is done to affect, or fix the moral and religious character of children, before the age of language than after; that the age of impressions, when parents are commonly waiting, in idle security, or trifling away their time in mischievous indiscretions, or giving up their children to the chance of such keeping as nurses and attendants may exercise, is in fact their golden opportunity; when more is likely to be done for their advantage or damage, than in all the instruction and discipline of their minority afterward.

And something like this I think we should augur before-hand, from the peculiar, full-born intensity of the maternal affection, at the moment when it first embraces the newly arrived object. It scarcely appears to grow, never to grow tender and self-sacrificing in its care. It turns itself to its charge, with a love that is boundless and fathomless, at the first. As if just then and there, some highest and most sacred office of motherhood were required to begin. Is it only that the child demands her physical nurture and carefulness? That is not the answer of her consciousness. Her maternity scorns all comparison with that of the mere animals. Her love, as she herself feels, looks through the body into the inborn person-ality of her child, — the man or woman to be. Nay, more than that, if she could sound her consciousness deeply enough, she would find a certain religiousness in it, measurable by no scale of mere earthly and temporal love. Here springs the secret of her maternity, and its semi-divine proportions. It is the call and equipment of God, for a work on the impression-al and plastic age of a soul. Christianized as it should be, and wrought in by the grace of the Spirit, the minuteness of its care, its gentleness, its patience, its almost divine faithfulness, are prepared for the shaping of a soul's immortality. And, to make the work a sure one, the intrusted soul is allowed to have no will as yet of its own, that this motherhood may more certainly plant the angel in the man, uniting him to all heavenly goodness by predispositions from itself, before he is united, as he will be, by choices of his own. Nothing but this explains and measures the wonderful proportions of maternity.

It will be seen at once, and will readily be taken as a confirmation of the transcendent importance of what is done, or possible to be done, for children, in their impressional and plastic age, that whatever is impressed or inserted here, at this early point, must be profoundly seminal, as regards all the future developments of the character. And though it can not, by the supposition, amount to character, in the responsible sense of that term, it may be the seed, in some very important sense, of all the future character to be unfolded; just as we familiarly think of sin itself, as a character in blame when the will is ripe, though prepared, in still another view, by the seminal damages and misaffections derived from sinning ancestors. So when a child, during the whole period of impressions, or passive recipiencies, previous to the development of his responsible will, lives in the life and feeling of his parents, and they in the molds of the Spirit, they will, of course, be shaping themselves in him, or him in themselves, and the effects wrought in him will be preparations of what he will by-and-bye do from himself; seeds, in that manner possible, even of a regenerate life and character.

That we may conceive this matter more adequately and exactly, consider, a moment, that whole contour of dispositions, affections, tempers, affinities, aspirations, which come into power in a soul after the will is set fast in a life of duty and devotion. These things, we conceive, follow in a sense the will, and then become in turn a new element about the will — a new heart, as we say, prompting to new acts and a continued life of new obedience. Now what I would affirm is, that just this same contour of dispositions and affinities may be prepared under, and come after, the will of the parents, when the child is living in their will, and be ready as a new element, or new heart, to prompt the child's will, or put it

forward in the choice of all duty, whenever it is so matured as
to choose for itself. Of course these regenerated dispositions
and affinities, this general disposedness to good, which we
call a new heart, supposes a work of the Spirit; and, if the
parents live in the Spirit as they ought, they will have the
Spirit for the child as truly as for themselves, and the child
will be grown, so to speak, in the molds of the Spirit, even
from his infancy.

This will be yet more probable, if we glance at some of the
particular facts and conditions involved. Thus if we speak of
impressions, or the age of impressions, and of that as an age
prior to language, what kind of religious impressions can be
raised in a soul, it may be asked, when the child is not far
enough developed in language to be taught any thing about
God, or Christ, or itself, that belongs to intelligence? And the
sufficient answer must be, that language itself has no meaning
till rudimental impressions are first begotten in the life of
experience, to give it a meaning. Words are useful to propagate meanings, or to farther develop and combine meanings,
but a child would never know the meaning of any word in a
language, just by hearing the sound of it in his ears. He must
learn to put the meaning into it, by having found that meaning
in his impressions, and then the word becomes significant.
And it requires a certain wakefulness and capacity of intelligent apprehension, to receive or take up such impressions. Thus a dog would never get hold of any religious
impression at the family prayers, all his lifetime; but a child
will be fast gathering up, out of his little life and experience,
impressional states and associations, that give meanings to
the words of prayer, as they, in turn, give meanings to the
facts of his experience. All language supposes impressions
first made. The word *light* does not signify any thing, till the
eye has taken the impression of light. The word *love* is un-
meaning, to one who has not loved and received love. The
word *God,* raises no conception of God, till the idea of such a
being has been somehow generated and associated with that
particular sound. How far off is it then from all sound appre-

hensions of fact, to imagine that nothing religious can be done for a child till after he is far enough developed in language to be taught; when in fact he could not be thus developed in language at all, if the meanings of language were not somehow started in him by the impressions derived from his experience.

Observe, again, how very quick the child's eye is, in the passive age of infancy, to catch impressions, and receive the meaning of looks, voices, and motions. It peruses all faces, and colors, and sounds. Every sentiment that looks into its eyes, looks back out of its eyes, and plays in miniature on its countenance. The tear that steals down the cheek of a mother's suppressed grief, gathers the little infantile face into a responsive sob. With a kind of wondering silence, which is next thing to adoration, it studies the mother in her prayer, and looks up piously with her, in that exploring watch, that signifies unspoken prayer. If the child is handled fretfully, scolded, jerked, or simply laid aside unaffectionately, in no warmth of motherly gentleness, it feels the sting of just that which is felt towards it; and so it is angered by anger, irritated by irritation, fretted by fretfulness; having thus impressed, just that kind of impatience or ill-nature, which is felt towards it, and growing faithfully into the bad mold offered, as by a fixed law. There is great importance, in this manner, even in the handling of infancy. If it is unchristian, it will beget unchristian states, or impressions. If it is gentle, even patient and loving, it prepares a mood and temper like its own. There is scarcely room to doubt, that all most crabbed, hateful, resentful, passionate, ill-natured characters; all most even, lovely, firm and true, are prepared, in a great degree, by the handling of the nursery. To these and all such modes of feeling and treatment as make up the element of the infant's life, it is passive as wax to the seal. So that if we consider how small a speck, falling into the nucleus of a crystal, may disturb its form; or, how even a mote of foreign matter present in the quickening egg, will suffice to produce a deformity; considering, also, on the other hand, what nice conditions of repose, in one case, and what accurately modulated supplies of heat in the other, are necessary to a perfect product; then only do we begin to imagine what work is going on, in the soul of a child, in this first chapter of life, the age of impressions.

It must also greatly affect our judgments on this point, to observe that, when this first age of impressions is gone by, there is, after that, no such thing any more as a possibility of absolute control. Thus far the child has been more a candidate for personality than a person. He has been as a seed forming in the capsule of the parent-stem, getting every thing from that stem, and fashioned, in its kind, by the fashioning kind of that. But now, having been gradually and imperceptibly ripened, as the seed separates and falls off, to be another and complete form of life in itself, so the child comes out, in his own power, a complete person, able to choose responsibly for himself. Now he is no more in the power of the parent, as before; the dominion of the older life is supplanted, by the self-asserting competency of the younger; what can the old stalk do upon the seed that is already ripe? The transition here is very gradual, it is true, covering even a space of years; and something may be done for the child's character by instruction, by the skillful management of motives, and the tender solicitudes of parental watching and prayer; but less and less, of course, the older the child becomes, and the more completely his personal responsibility is developed. But how very fearful the change, and how much it means, that the child, once plastic and passive to the will of the parent, has gotten by the point of absolute disposability, and is never again to be properly in that will! The perilous power of self-care and self-assertion has come, and what is to be the result? And how much does it signify to the parent, when he feels his power to be thus growing difficult, weak, doubtful, or finally quite ended! What a conception it is, that he once had his child in absolute direction, and the fashioning of his own superior will, to dress, to feed, to handle, to play himself into his sentiments, be the disposition of his dispositions, the temper of his tempers. Was there not something great to be done then, when the advantage was so great — now to be done no more? It will be difficult to shake off that impression; impossible to a really thoughtful Christian soul. And if the will, now matured and gone over into complete self-assertion, rushes into all wildness and profligacy, unrestrained and unrestrainable, the recollection of a time when it was restrainable and could have been molded, even as wax itself, will return with inevitable certainty upon the parents, and taunt, O how bitterly, the neglectfulness and lightness, by which they cast their opportunity away!

I bring into view accordingly, just here, a consideration that goes further to establish the position I am asserting, than any other, and one that is naturally suggested by the topic just adverted to. We call this first chapter of life the age of impressions; we speak of the child as being in a sense passive and plastic, living in the will of the parents, having no will developed for responsible action. It might be imagined from the use of such terms, that the infant or very young child has no will at all. But that is not any true conception. It has no *responsible* will, because it is not acquainted, as yet, with those laws and limits and conditions of choice that make it responsible. Nevertheless it has will, blind will, as strongly developed as any other faculty, and sometimes even most strongly of all. The manifestations of it are sometimes even frightful. And precisely this it is which makes the age of impressions, the age prior to language and responsible choice, most profoundly critical in its importance. It is the age in which the will-power of the soul is to be tamed or subordinated to a higher control; that of obedience to parents, that of duty and religion. And, in this view, it is that every thing most important to the religious character turns just here. Is this infant child to fill the universe with his complete and total self-assertion, owning no superior, or is he to learn the self-submission of allegiance, obedience, duty to God? Is he to become a demon let loose in God's eternity or an angel and free prince of the realm?

That he may be this, he is now given, will and all, as wax, to the wise molding-power of control. Beginning, then, to lift his will in mutiny, and swell in self-asserting obstinacy, refusing to go or come, or stand, or withhold in this or that, let there be no fight begun, or issue made with him, as if it were the true thing now to break his will, or drive him out of it by mere terrors and pains. This willfulness, or obstinacy, is not so purely bad, or evil, as it seems. It is partly his feeling of himself and you, in which he is getting hold of the conditions of authority, and feeling out his limitations. No, this breaking of a child's will to which many well-meaning parents set themselves, with such instant, almost passionate resolution, is the way they take to make him a coward, or a thief, or a hypocrite, or a mean-spirited and driveling sycophant — nothing in fact is more dreadful to thought than this breaking of a will, when it breaks, as it often does, the personality itself, and all highest, noblest firmness of manhood. The true problem is different; it is not to break, but to bend rather, to draw the will down, or away from self-assertion toward self-devotion, to teach it the way of submitting to wise limitations, to raise it into the great and glorious liberties of a state of loyalty to God. See then how it is to be done. The child has no force, however stout he is in his will. Take him up then, when the fit is upon him, carry him, stand him on his feet, set him here or there, do just that in him which he refuses to do in himself — all this gently and kindly as if he were capable of maintaining no issue at all. Do it again and again, as often as may be necessary. By-and-bye, he will begin to perceive that his obstinacy is but the fussing of his weakness; till finally, as the sense of limitation comes up into a sense of law and duty, he will be found to have learned, even beforehand, the folly of mere self-assertion. And when he has reached this point of felt obligation to obedience it will no longer break him down to enforce his compliance, but it will even exalt into greater dignity and capacity, that sublime power of self-government, by which his manhood is to be most distinguished.

By a different treatment at the point or crisis just named, that is by raising an issue to be driven straight through by terror and storm, one of two results almost equally bad were likely to follow; the child would either have been quite broken down by fear, the lowest of all possible motives when separated from moral convictions, or else would have been made a hundred fold more obstinate by his triumph. Nature provided for his easy subjugation, by putting him in the hands of a superior strength, which could manage him without any fight of enforcement — to have him schooled and tempered to a customary self-surrender which takes nothing from his natural force and manliness. And so is accomplished what, in one view, is the great problem of life; that on which all duty and allegiance to God, in the state even of conversion, depends.

It only remains to add that we are not to assume the comparative unimportance of what is done upon a child, in his age of impressions, because there is really no character of virtue or vice, or blame or praise, developed in that age. Be it so — it is so by the supposition. But the power, the root, the seed, is implanted nevertheless, in most cases, of what he will be. Not in every case, but often, the seed of a regenerate life is implanted — that which makes the child a Christian in God's view, as certainly as if he were already out in the testimony and formal profession of his faith. I was just now speaking of the dreadful power of will or willfulness, some times manifested even in this first age, that we have called the age of impressions, and of the ways in which, by one kind of mismanagement or another, the character may be turned to vices that are as opposite, as the vices of meanness and the crimes of violence and blood. So it will be found that almost every sort of mismanagement, or neglect, plants some seed of vice and misery that grows out afterwards into a character in its own kind. Thus the child by a continual worry of his little life, under abusive words, and harsh, flashy tempers, grows to be a bed of nettles in all his personal tempers, and will so be prepared to break out, in the age of choice, into almost any vice of ill-nature. A child can be pampered in feeding, so as to become, in a sense, all body; so that, when he comes into choice and responsible action, he is already a confirmed sensualist, showing it in the lines of his face, even before it appears in his tastes, habits and vices. Thus we have a way of wondering that the children of this or that family should turn out so poorly, but the real fact is, probably, if we knew it, that what we call their turning out, is only their growing out, in just that which was first grown in, by the mismanagement of their infancy and childhood. What they took in as impression, or contagion, is developed by choice — not at once, perhaps, but finally, after the poison has had time to work. And in just the same way, doubtless, it may be true, in multitudes of Christian conversions, that what appear to be such to others, and also to the subjects themselves, are only the restored activity and more fully developed results of some predispositional state, or initially sanctified property, in the tempers and subtle affinities of their childhood. They are now born into that by the assent of their own will, which they were in before, without their will. What they do not remember still remembers them, and now claims a right in them. What was before unconscious, flames out into consciousness, and they break forth into praise and thanksgiving, in that which, long ago, took them initially, and touched them softly without thanks. For there is such a thing as a seed of character in religion, preceding all religious development. Even as Calvin, speaking of the regenerative grace there may be in the heart of infancy itself, testifies — "the work of God is not yet without existence, because it is not observed and understood by us."

By these and many other considerations that might be named, it is made clear, I think, to any judicious and thoughtful person, that the most important age of Christian nurture is the first; that which we have called the age of impressions, just that age, in which the duties and cares of a really Christian nurture are so commonly postponed, or assumed to have not yet arrived. I have no scales to measure quantities of effect in this matter of early training, but I may be allowed to express my solemn conviction, that more, as a general fact, is done, or lost by neglect of doing, on a child's immortality, in the first three years of his life, than in all his years of discipline afterwards. And I name this particular time, or date, that I may not be supposed to lay the chief stress of duty and care on the latter part of what I have called the age of impressions; which, as it is a matter somewhat indefinite, may be taken to cover the space of three or four times this number of years; the development of language, and of moral ideas being only partially accomplished, in most cases, for so long a time. Let every Christian father and mother understand, when their child is three years old, that they have done more than half of all they will ever do for his character. What can be more strangely wide of all just apprehension, than the immense efficacy, imputed by most parents to the Christian ministry, compared with what they take to be the almost insignificant power conferred on them in their parental charge and duties. Why, if all preachers of Christ could have their hearers, for whole months and years, in their own will, as parents do their children, so as to move them by a look, a motion, a smile, a frown, and act their own sentiments and emotions over in them at pleasure; if also, a little farther on, they had them in authority to command, direct, tell them whither to go, what to learn, what to do, regulate their hours, their books, their pleasures, their company, and call them to prayer over their own knees every night and morning, who could think it impossible, in the use of such a power, to produce almost any result? Should not such a ministry be expected to fashion all who come under it to newness of life? Let no parent, shifting off his duties to his children, in this manner, think to have his defects made up, and the consequent damages mended afterwards, when they have come to their maturity, by the comparatively slender, always doubtful, efficacy of preaching and pulpit harangue.

If now I am right in the view I have been trying to establish, it will readily occur to you that irreparable damage may be and must often be done by the self-indulgence of those parents, who place their children mostly in the charge of nurses and attendants for just those years of their life, in which the greatest and most absolute effects are to be wrought in their character. The lightness that prevails, on this point, is really astonishing. Many parents do not even take pains to know any thing about the tempers, the truthfulness, the character generally, of the nurses to whom their children are thus confidingly trusted. No matter—the child is too young to be poisoned, or at all hurt, by their influence. And so they give over, to these faithless and often cruelly false hirelings of the nursery, to be always with them, under their power, associated with their persons, handled by their roughness, and imprinted, day and night, by the coarse, bad sentiments of their voices and faces, these helpless, hapless beings whom they call their children, and think they are really making much of, in the instituting of a nursery for them and their keeping. Such a mother ought to see that she is making much more of herself than of her child. This whole scheme of nurture is a scheme of self-indulgence. Now is the time when her little one most needs to see her face, and hear her voice, and feel her gentle hand. Now is the time when her child's eternity pleads most entreatingly for the benefit of her motherly charge and presence. What mother would not be dismayed by the thought of having her family grow up into the sentiments of her nurse, and come forward into life as being in the succession to her character! And yet how often is this most exactly what she has provided for.

Again, it is very clear that, in this early kind of nurture, faithfully maintained, there is a call for the greatest personal holiness in the parents, and that just those conditions are added, which will make true holiness closest to nature, and most beautifully attractive—saving it from all the repulsive appearances of severity and sanctimony. In this charge and nurture of infant children, nothing is to be done by an artificial, lecturing process; nothing, or little by what can be called government. We are to get our effects chiefly by just being what we ought, and making a right presence of love and life to our children. They are in a plastic age that is receiving its type, not from our words, but from our spirit, and whose character is shaping in the molds of ours. Living under this conviction, we are held to a sound verity and reality in every thing. The defect of our character is not to be made up here, by the sanctity of our words; we must be all that we would have our children feel and receive. Thus, if a man were to be set before a mirror, with the feeling that the exact image of what he *is*, for the day, is there to be produced and left as a permanent and fixed image forever, to what carefulness, what delicate sincerity of spirit would he be moved. And will he be less moved to the same, when that mirror is the soul of his child?

Inducted, thus, into a more profoundly real holiness, we shall, at the same time, grow more natural in it. The family quality of our piety, living itself into our children, will moisten the dry individualism we suffer, relieve the eccentricities we display, set purity in the place of bustle and presumption, growth in the place of conquest, sound health in the place of spasmodic exaltations; for when a conviction is felt in Christian families, that living is to be a means of grace, and as God will suffer it, a regenerating power, then will our piety become a domestic spirit, and as much more tender, as it is closer to the life of childhood. Now, we have a kind of piety that contains, practically speaking, only adults, or those who are old enough to reflect and act for themselves, and it is as if we lived in an *adult world,* where every one is for himself. If we could abolish also distinctions of age, and sex, and office, we should only make up a style of religion somewhat drier and farther off from nature than we now have. We can never come into the true mode of living that God has appointed for us, until we regard each generation as hovering over the next, acting itself into the next, and casting thus a type of character in the next, before it comes to act for itself. Then we shall have gentle cares and feelings; then the families will become bonds of spiritual life; example, education and government, being Christian powers, will be regulated by Christian spirit;

the rigidities of religious principle will be softened by the tender affections of nature twining among them, and the common life of the house dignified by the sober and momentous cares of the life to come. And thus Christian piety, being oftener a habit in the soul than a conquest over it, will be as much more respectable and consistent as it is earlier in the birth and closer to nature.

• • • • •

V.   FAMILY GOVERNMENT

• • • • •

Family Government, then, is the subject here suggested for discussion. And we naturally endeavor—

I. *To ascertain what is the true conception of family government.*

Of course it is to be government; about that there ought to be no hesitation. It is not to be a mere nursing, or dressing, or provisioning agency; not to be an exhorting, advising, consulting relationship; not to be a lavishing of devotion, or parental self-sacrifice; but the radical constitutive idea, that in which it becomes family government, is that it governs, uses authority, maintains law and rules, by a binding and loosing power, over the moral nature of the child. Parents, it would sometimes appear, fall into a practical ambiguity here—as if the governing power were a kind of severity, or harsh assumption; not perceiving that, by common consent, we speak of an ungoverned family as the synonym of a disorderly, wretched, and dishonored, if not ruined, family. There is no greater cruelty, in fact, than this same false tenderness, which is the bane of so many families. There is a kind of cruelty indeed, which is exactly opposite, and misses the idea of government on the other side, viz: that brutish manner of despotic will and violence, which makes no appeal to the moral nature at all, driving straight by, upon the fears, in a battery of force. And yet, whether even this be really more

cruel in its effects, than the false tenderness just named, is a
fair subject of doubt. The true idea, that which makes the
domestic order and state so beneficent, is that it is to be a
state of government; a state where love has authority, and
presides in the beneficent order of law.

• • • • •

First of all, their family government is never conceived, in
its true nature, except when it is regarded as a vice-gerent
authority, set up by God, and ruling in his place. Instead of
creating us outright, God has seen fit to give us existence
under laws of reproduction; having it for his object, in the
family order and relationship, to set us forth, under a kind of
experience in the small, and in terms of sense, that faithfully
typifies our wider relationship to Him, the eternal Father and
invisible Ruler of the worlds. We are infants too, men and
women in the small, that we may be as flexible in our will as
possible. Our parents, if they are godly themselves, as by the
supposition they will be, are to personate God, in the double
sense of bearing his natural and moral image before us, ever
close at hand; and also in the right of authority with which
they are clothed. And, that they may have us at the greatest
advantage, it is given them to clothe us, and feed us, and
bathe us, day and night, in the unsparing and lavish attentions
of their love; enjoying our enjoyments, and even their own
sacrifices for us. First, the mother has us, at her bosom, as a
kind of nursing Providence. Perused by touch and by the
eyes, her soul of maternity, watching for that look and bending ever to it, raises the initial sense of a divine something in
the world; and when she begins to speak her soft imperative,
putting a little decision into the tones of her love, she makes
the first and gentlest possible beginning of authority. And
then the stiffer tension of the masculine word, connected
with the wider, rougher providence of a father's masculine
force, follows in a stouter mode of authority, and the moral
nature of the child, configured thereto, answers faithfully in a
rapidly developed sense of obligation. The parents are to fill,

in this manner, an office strictly religious; personating God in the child's feeling and conscience, and bending it, thus, to what, without any misnomer, we call a filial piety. So that when the unseen Father and Lord is Himself discovered, there is to be a piety made ready for him; a kind of house-religion, that may widen out into the measures of God's ideal majesty and empire. Hence the injunction, "Children obey your parents in the Lord." They could not make a beginning with ideas of God, or with God as an unseen Spirit; therefore they had parents given them in the Lord – the Lord to be in them, there to personate and finite himself, and gather to such human motherhood and fatherhood, a piety transferable to Himself, as the knowledge of his nobler, unseen Fatherhood arrives. . . .

• • • • •

Closely related is the conviction to be firmly held, that family discipline, rightly administered, is to secure, and may secure, a style of obedience in the child that amounts to a real piety. If we speak of conversion, family government should be a converting ordinance, as truly as preaching. For observe and make due account of this single fact, that when a child is brought to do any one thing from a truly right motive, and in a genuinely right spirit, there is implied in that kind of obedience, the acceptance of all best and holiest principle. I do not mean, of course, that children are to be made Christians by the rod, or by any summary process of requirement. There is no such short method of compulsory piety here, as some are reported to have held, or put in exercise. But it is not absurd to expect and aim to realize in the family, a genuine spirit of obedience; obedience, that is, from the principle that God enthrones, and which underlies all piety – just what the apostle means, if I understand him rightly, by having children "in subjection with all gravity." In the phrase "all gravity," he is looking at a kind of obedience that touches the deepest notes of principle and character. Contrary to this, there is an obedience without principle, which is obedience with all levity; that which is paid to mere will and force; that which is another name for fear; that which is bought by promises and paid by indulgences; that which makes a time-server, or a coward, or a lying pretender, as the case may be, and not a Christian. This latter—that which makes a Christian—is the aim of all true government, and should never be out of sight for an hour. Let the child be brought to do right because it is right, and not because it is unsafe, or appears badly, to do wrong. In every case of discipline for ill-nature, wrong, will-fulness, disobedience, be it understood, that the real point is carried never till the child is gentled into love and duty; sorry, in all heartiness, for the past, with a glad mind set to the choice of doing right and pleasing God. How often is it true that in the successful carrying of such a point, (which can not be carried, save by great resources of love and gospel life in the parents,) the fact of a converted will is gained. And one must be a dull observer of children and their after life, who has not many times suspected that just the ones who are said to be converted afterwards, and suppose themselves to be, had their wills, not seldom bowed to this in their childhood, under the government of the house.

• • • • •

. . . Let there be only such and so many things command-ed, as can be faithfully attended to—these in a gentle and firm voice, as if their title to obedience lay in their own merit—and then let the child be held to a perfectly inevitable and faithful account; and, by that time, it will be seen that order and law have a stress of their own, and a power to rule in their own divine right. The beauty of a well-governed family will be seen, in this manner, to be a kind of silent, natural-looking power; as if it were a matter only of growth, and could never have been otherwise.

At first, or in the earlier periods of childhood, authority should rest upon its own right, and expect to be obeyed just because it speaks. It should stake itself on no assigned rea-sons, and have nothing to do with reasons, unless it be after the fact; when, by showing what has been depending, in a manner unseen to the child, it can add a presumption of reason to all future commands. It is even a good thing to the moral and religious nature of a child, to have its obedience required, and to be accustomed to obedience, on the ground of simple authority; to learn homage and trust, as all subject natures must, and so to accept the rule of God's majesty, when the reasons of God are inscrutable. There is little prospect that any child will be a Christian, or any thing but a skeptic, or a godless worldling, who has not had his religious nature unfolded by an early subjection to authority, speaking in its own right.

Nay, I will go farther; there is a certain use in having a child, in the first stages of government, feel the pressure of law as a restriction. For, as the law of God is a schoolmaster to bring us to Christ, so there is a like relation between law and liberty in the training of the house. It is by a certain friction, if I may so speak, on the moral nature, a certain pressure of control, not always welcome, that the sense of law gets hold of us. Observances that we do not like, prepare us to a kind of obedience, further on, that is free — that welcomes the same command because it is good, the same authority because it is wholesome and right. And so it comes to pass that a son, grown almost to manhood, will gladly serve the house, and yield to his parents a kind of homage that even anticipates their wishes, just because he has learned to be in subjection, with all gravity, under restrictions that were once a sore limit on his patience.

At the same time it should never be forgotten, in this due assertion of authority and restrictive law, that there is a great difference between the imperative and the dictatorial; between the exact and the exacting. I have spoken already of the common fault of commanding overmuch, and forgetting or omitting to enforce what is commanded; there is another kind of fault which commands overmuch, and rigidly exacts what is commanded; laying on commands, as it seems to the child, just because it can, or is willing to gall his peace by exacting something that shall cut away even the semblance of liberty.

No parent has a right to put oppression on a child, in the name of authority. And if he uses authority in that way, to annoy the child's peace, and even to forbid his possession of himself, he should not complain, if the impatience he creates grows into a bitter animosity, and finally a stiff rebellion. Nothing should ever be commanded except what is needed and required by the most positive reasons, whether those reasons are made known or not.

Another qualification here to be observed, belongs to what may be called the emancipation of the child. A wise parent understands that his government is to be crowned by an act of emancipation; and it is a great problem, to accomplish that emancipation gracefully. Pure authority, up to the last limit of minority, then a total, instantaneous self-possession, makes an awkward transition. A young eagle kept in the nest and brooded over till his beak and talons are full-grown, then pitched out of it and required to take care of himself, will most certainly be dashed upon the ground. The emancipating process, in order to be well finished, should begin early, and should pass imperceptibly, even as age increases imperceptibly. Thus the child, after being ruled for a time, by pure authority, should begin, as the understanding is developed, to have some of the reasons given why it is required to abstain, or do, or practice, in this or that way instead of some other. The tastes of the child, too, should begin to be a little consulted, in respect to his school, his studies, his future engagements in life. When he is old enough to go on errands, and to labor in various employments for the benefit of the family, he should be let into the condition of the family far enough to be identified with it, and have the family cause, and property, and hope, for his own. Built into the family fortunes and sympathies, in this manner, he will begin, at a very early day, to command himself for it, and so will get ready to command himself for himself, in a way that will be just as if the parental authority were still running on, after it has quite run by.

• • • • •

BOOK MANUFACTURE

Child-Rearing Concepts, 1628–1861: Historical Sources was composed by Allied Typesetting and Publishing Company, Dexter, Michigan, with printing and binding by NAPCO Graphic Arts, Inc., New Berlin, Wisconsin. The cover design was by Evelyn Hansen; internal design was by F. E. Peacock Publishers, Inc., art department. The type is Times Roman.